Visual Science Encyclopedia

Heat
and
Energy

▲ The bright blue flame of a camping stove burning butane—just one of a wide range of gases extracted from natural gas, which is, itself, just one of many sources of energy that we use.

How to use this book

Every word defined in this book can be found in alphabetical order on pages 3 to 47. There is also a full index on page 48. A number of other features will help you get the most out of the *Visual Science Encyclopedia*. They are shown below.

Here you will find the first word defined on any left-hand page.

Each word is shown in bold so it is easy to find.

Other words defined in the book are highlighted in bold.

Plus, many entries point to related words of interest.

Here you will find the last word defined on any right-hand page.

Each new letter of the alphabet is clearly marked to help you find the word you are looking for quicker.

Illustrations for some words complement the text and provide further information on a topic.

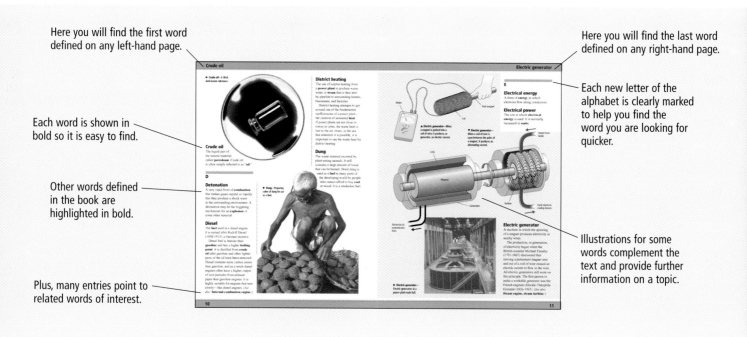

Acknowledgments

Grolier Educational
First published in the United States in 2002 by Grolier Educational, Sherman Turnpike, Danbury, CT 06816

Copyright © 2002
Atlantic Europe Publishing Company Ltd.

Author
Brian Knapp, BSc, PhD

Art Director
Duncan McCrae, BSc

Senior Designer
Adele Humphries, BA, PGCE

Editors
Lisa Magloff, BA, and Mary Sanders, BSc

Illustrations
David Woodroffe

Designed and produced by
EARTHSCAPE EDITIONS

Reproduced in Malaysia by
Global Color

Printed in Hong Kong by
Wing King Tong Company Ltd.

Library of Congress Cataloging-in-Publication Data
Visual Science Encyclopedia
   p. cm.
   Includes indexes.
   Contents: v. 1. Weather—v. 2.
Elements—v. 3. Rocks, minerals, and soil—
v. 4. Forces—v. 5. Light and sound—
v. 6. Water—v. 7. Plants—v. 8. Electricity
and magnetism—v. 9. Earth and space—
v. 10. Computers and the Internet—v. 11.
Earthquakes and volcanoes—v. 12. Heat
and energy.
   ISBN 0-7172-5595-6 (set: alk. paper)—ISBN
0-7172-5596-4 (v. 1: alk. paper)—ISBN
0-7172-5597-2 (v. 2: alk. paper)—ISBN
0-7172-5598-0 (v. 3: alk. paper)—ISBN
0-7172-5599-9 (v. 4: alk. paper)—ISBN
0-7172-5600-6 (v. 5: alk. paper)—ISBN
0-7172-5601-4 (v. 6: alk. paper)—ISBN
0-7172-5602-2 (v. 7: alk. paper)—ISBN
0-7172-5603-0 (v. 8: alk. paper)—ISBN
0-7172-5604-9 (v. 9: alk. paper)—ISBN
0-7172-5605-7 (v. 10: alk. paper)—ISBN
0-7172-5606-5 (v. 11: alk. paper)—ISBN
0-7172-5607-3 (v. 12: alk. paper)
   1. Science—Encyclopedias, Juvenile.
[1. Science—Encyclopedias.] I. Grolier
Educational (Firm)

QI21.V58 2001
503—dc21
                                    2001023704

Picture credits
All photographs are from the Earthscape Editions photolibrary except the following:
(c=center t=top b=bottom l=left r=right)

The British Coal Corporation 17b;
BP International 33; *Fire Research Station* 7tr;
NASA 26bl.

This product is manufactured from sustainable managed forests. For every tree cut down, at least one more is planted.

A

Acid rain

A form of **pollution** produced when gases, mainly given off during the production of electric **power** in **power plants**, dissolve in rainwater and turn it into dilute acids. The most common gas waste is sulfur dioxide, and the most common type of rain is dilute sulfurous acid. This acid can get into the soil and affect plant growth. It can also mix with fresh water, making it impossible for fish and many other creatures to live.

Atomic energy

(*See:* **Nuclear energy**.)

B

Battery

A portable device for converting **chemical energy** into **electrical energy**. Strictly speaking, a battery is made of two or more cells. However, many people use the words cell and battery interchangeably. (*See also:* **Electrochemical cell** and **Fuel cell**.)

When a battery is connected to a device like a light bulb, there is an unseen flow of tiny particles called electrons, which creates electricity (an electric current).

Batteries were invented by Alessandro Volta around 1800. All batteries contain two different materials separated by a paste or a liquid. The chemical reaction that occurs releases electrons.

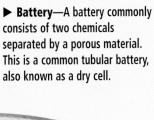

▶ **Battery**—A battery commonly consists of two chemicals separated by a porous material. This is a common tubular battery, also known as a dry cell.

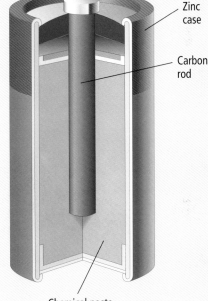

Zinc case

Carbon rod

Chemical paste

100°C Boiling point of water

Bubbles inside boiling water

Boiling point

The temperature at which a substance changes into a gas. The boiling point of water is 100°C. (*See also:* **Heat of vaporization** and **Steam**.)

◀ **Boiling point**—The boiling point occurs when water has enough energy to vaporize inside the liquid, not just off the surface. When this happens, bubbles form inside the liquid and rise violently to the surface.

Brown coal

An alternative word for **lignite**.

Burning

A form of **combustion** in which a **flame** is produced. A flame occurs where gases combust and release **heat** and **light**. At least two gases are therefore required if there is to be a flame. For example, **natural gas** burns in oxygen gas to produce **carbon dioxide** and water.

C

Caloric theory

In the 18th century caloric was thought to be a weightless fluid that was involved when **heat** was transferred from one object to another. It was assumed that it was lost to the air during **combustion**. In time it was shown that only **energy** is transferred, not any kind of material.

Calorie (cal)

A unit of **energy** or **heat**. One calorie is equal to 4.2 **joules**. It is used in a wide range of areas. In common use it refers to the heating value of food, creating a standard way of comparing foods to assess their energy value. The **food energy** value can then be compared to the amount of heat energy a body needs to be healthy. An excess of calories compared to

Tomato contains vitamins

Meat contains fat

Roll contains carbohydrates

the body's needs is likely to result in people becoming fat; too few food calories is likely to result in a person losing weight.

Carbohydrate

A group containing two common types of substance found in food: sugars and starches. The word carbohydrate literally means carbon and water. Carbohydrates are the most common materials and the main **energy** sources in living things. They are formed by green plants, using **carbon dioxide** gas in the air and water during **photosynthesis**.

There are several kinds of sugars. The simpler sugars (which occur in fruit and honey) are easily broken down in the body, and the energy in them is released quickly.

◄ **Carbohydrate**—The roll part of this hamburger is carbohydrate. The meat contains fat, which also has energy.

◄ **Burning**—Combustion with a flame. This is a garden bonfire.

Mother's milk also contains quick-releasing energy of this kind.

More complex sugars are found in sugar beet and sugarcane. They are used to make granulated sugar. A special form of carbohydrate called glycogen is made in the liver and muscles. It is stored there as a source of energy to be used, for example, when we run fast and need energy in our muscles.

The more complex kinds of sugars (called polysaccharides) are very large molecules and are used as a long-term supply of energy. Starch is an example of this type of sugar. Starch is found mostly in the seeds, roots, and stems of plants. We eat starch in bread, pasta, potatoes, rice, and other foods. (*See also:* **Food energy**.)

Carbon dioxide

A gas released as the result of **combustion** of **fuels**. It is the gas that flows out of the lungs during breathing, as well as the gas released by **power plants** when **fossil fuels** are burned. Carbon dioxide is needed by plants for growing tissues. (*See also:* **Carbohydrate**; **Greenhouse effect**; **Pollution**.)

Change of state

All substances can exist in three states: solid, liquid, and gas. A change of state is the physical change in a substance as a result of **heat** being added or taken away. For example, a substance can change from a liquid to a gas as a result of adding heat **energy**. It can change from a liquid to a solid as a result of a loss of heat energy. (*See also:* **Boiling point**; **Condensation**; **Evaporation**; **Freezing point**; **Latent heat**; **Melting point**; **Vaporization**.)

Charcoal

An impure form of graphite. It is made by **burning** wood in a kiln where there is limited access to air. Charcoal is similar to **coke** (which is **coal** burned in a limited supply of air). That is why the charcoal **fuel** that was traditionally for iron-making blast furnaces could be replaced by coke.

Charcoal is made by laying out a tall pile of thin, dry branches, leaving a space in the center that can act as a chimney. The pile is covered with soil, clay, or other materials that will retain the **heat** and keep out air. A fire is set in the bottom of the chimney, and as soon as the wood begins to burn, the top of the chimney is closed so that air can no longer flow freely through the pile. The wood continues to **smolder** for many days or weeks until it has all turned to charcoal. At this stage the covering material is removed and the charcoal bagged and sold as a source of smokeless fuel. Charcoal is still widely used as a fuel throughout the developing world because it produces a higher temperature **flame** than wood and burns more slowly.

Chemical energy

A form of **potential energy** stored as chemicals. For example, there are two chemicals in a **battery**. The battery is therefore a source of chemical energy. When the battery is put into a circuit, the chemical energy is changed to **electrical energy**. Food is also a form of chemical energy, which is released when the food is digested (*see:* **Food energy**). Fireworks and bombs are more dramatic examples of chemical energy. (*See also:* **Fuel cell**.)

▼ **Charcoal**—Charcoal being made in Madagascar. Wooden sticks are allowed to smolder for days under an earth pile. The demand for charcoal has stripped the nearby hills of their forest cover.

▶ **Chemical energy**— A firework contains energy in the form of dry chemicals. Fireworks are a mixture of 75% potassium nitrate, 15% carbon, and 10% sulfur. Small amounts of chemicals add color. This is the same recipe as for gunpowder.

Coal

A black, carbon-rich material made by compacting and heating plant remains over millions of years. It is one of the most important **fossil fuels**. Coal is now mainly used for generating electricity. In the past coal was used to **power steam engines**, to make gases for use in home lighting and cooking (before **natural gas** was discovered), and as direct heating in homes. Coal can be burned under controlled conditions to produce the smokeless **fuel** called **coke**.

Coke

A cindery material left behind when **coal** is heated to a high temperature out of contact with air. Coke is nearly pure carbon. It is used as a smokeless **fuel** and in industrial furnaces. Large amounts are used, for example, in **smelting** iron.

▲▼ **Coal**—Coal is one of the main sources of fossil fuel energy. More and more coal is being mined in deep pits (called open-pit mining), rather than using more dangerous underground mining techniques.

◄ **Coke**—Coke is a form of graphite used in furnaces because of the high temperature at which it burns.

▲ **Combustion**—This room has caught on fire due to a smoldering cigarette left on a chair. Because flames are produced, this form of combustion is called burning.

Combustion

When two substances react together to release **heat** and sometimes **light**. Some combustion reactions are slow, such as the combustion of the sugar we eat to provide our **energy** (*see:* **Food energy**). If the combustion is faster and results in a **flame**, it is called **burning**. A flame occurs where gases combust and release heat and light. Very rapid combustion results in **detonation** and **explosion**.

◄ **Combustion**—When copper is put into chlorine gas, combustion begins. No flames are produced during this process, so the copper does not burn.

Burning can be triggered by a source of heat, such as a spark or a flame, or simply from an increase in heat, for example, near an intense fire, even though the gases combusting are well clear of the source of flames. Oxygen is usually one of the substances in the reaction. (*See also:* **Exothermic reaction**; **Internal combustion engine**; **Smolder**.)

Condensation

The **change of state** from a gas to a liquid at any temperature above the **freezing point** due to **heat** being taken from the gas.

▶ **Condensation**—Water changing state from gas back to a liquid and condensing inside a bottle.

Conduction

The passing of **energy** between substances as a result of their being in contact. For example, **heat** energy is passed by contact from a hot substance to a cold one (such as when a pan is placed on a stove).

Sound energy is passed through walls, floors, and ceilings by conduction. Sound energy also moves through the eardrum and the bones of the middle ear by conduction. (*See also:* **Convection; Heat transfer; Radiation.**)

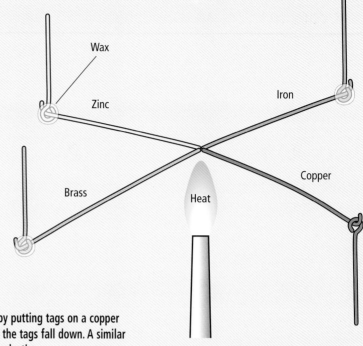

▼▶ **Conduction**—The progress of heat conduction can be demonstrated by putting tags on a copper rod with paraffin wax. As the heat moves along the rod, the wax melts, and the tags fall down. A similar demonstration (right) shows that different metals have different rates of conduction.

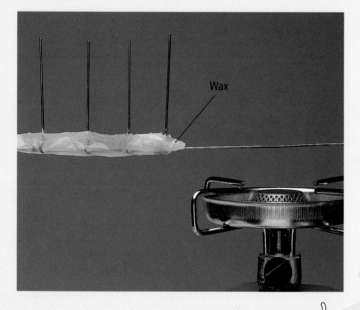

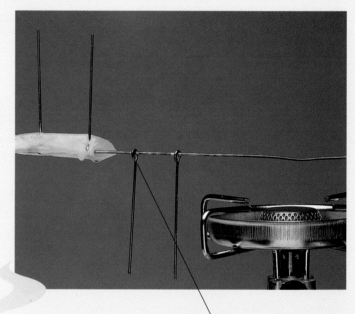

As the metal conducts heat along its length, it melts the wax, and the short wire tags swing free. The better the metal is at conducting heat, the quicker this will happen.

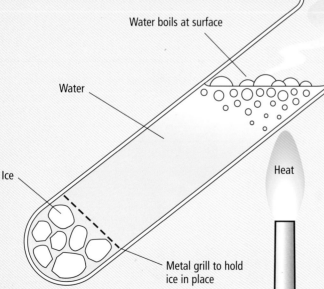

◀ **Conduction**—Water is a poor conductor of heat. That can be shown by placing an ice cube in the bottom of a boiling tube, and then heating the top part of the tube until the water boils. The ice will not melt.

Conservation of energy

The basic scientific idea that **energy** is never created or destroyed, but simply changed from one form to another. For example, if **fuel wood** is burned, **chemical energy** is converted into **heat** energy. When the wood has burned away, the amount of chemical energy that was in the wood has all been turned into other forms of energy, such as heat, **light**, and **sound**. Thus, it is never strictly true to say that energy is used up. This is different from the common way of talking about energy conservation. When energy is described as being used up, what is really meant is that the form of energy useful to us is gone and has been turned into low-level heat that we can no longer use. (*See also:* **Conservation of mass; Energy conversion; Heat conservation.**)

Conservation of mass

The idea that mass is neither created or destroyed, but only changed from one form to another. For example, when a liquid is heated, it changes to a gas but the mass of gas is the same as the mass of liquid.

Einstein's theory of relativity shows that mass is related to **energy** for objects traveling close to the speed of **light** ($e = mc^2$, where e = energy, m = mass, and c = the speed of light).

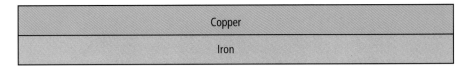

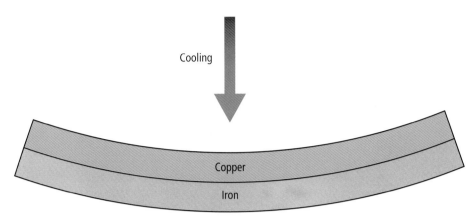

▲ **Contraction**—Copper and iron have different rates of contraction and expansion. If strips of the two metals are fastened together and then cooled, the copper contracts (gets shorter) faster and makes the strips curve.

Contraction

The decrease in the size of an object when it is cooled. It is the opposite of **expansion**.

Convection

The transfer of **energy** through a liquid or a gas by means of its circulation (*see:* **Heat transfer**).

For example, when a pan of water is heated on a stove, the lower layers of the liquid become hot first (because of **conduction**). This hot liquid is less dense than the cooler liquid above it and rises to the surface. Some of the cooler liquid takes its place. This movement sets up a circulation of water. The circulation is convection.

Converting energy

(*See:* **Energy conversion.**)

Cooling system

(*See:* **Heat exchanger.**)

▶ **Convection**—This can be shown by putting a few permanganate of potash crystals on a heater in a tank. The circulation of water due to convection soon begins.

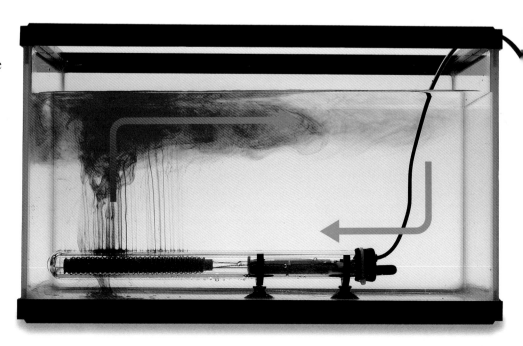

Crude oil

▶ **Crude oil**—A thick, dark-brown substance.

Crude oil
The liquid part of the natural material called **petroleum**. Crude oil is often simply referred to as "**oil**."

D

Detonation
A very rapid form of **combustion** that makes gases expand so rapidly that they produce a shock wave in the surrounding environment. A detonation may be the triggering mechanism for an **explosion** of some other material.

Diesel
The **fuel** used in a diesel engine. It is named after Rudolf Diesel (1858-1913), a German inventor.

Diesel fuel is heavier than **gasoline** and has a higher **boiling point**. It is distilled from **crude oil** after gasoline and other lighter parts of the oil have been removed. Diesel contains more carbon atoms than gasoline, and as a result diesel engines often have a higher output of soot particles from exhaust pipes than gasoline engines. It is highly suitable for engines that turn slowly—like diesel engines. (*See also:* **Internal combustion engine**.)

District heating
The use of surplus heating from a **power plant** to produce warm water or **steam** that is then sent by pipeline to surrounding homes, businesses, and factories.

District heating attempts to get around one of the fundamental inefficiencies of a power plant—the creation of unwanted **heat**. If power plants are not close to towns or cities, the waste heat is lost to the air, rivers, or the sea. But wherever it is possible, it is important to use the waste heat for district heating.

Dung
The waste material excreted by plant-eating animals. It still contains a large amount of tissue that can be burned. Dried dung is used as a **fuel** in many parts of the developing world by people who cannot afford to buy **coal** or wood. It is a smokeless fuel.

▶ **Dung**—Preparing cakes of dung for use as a fuel.

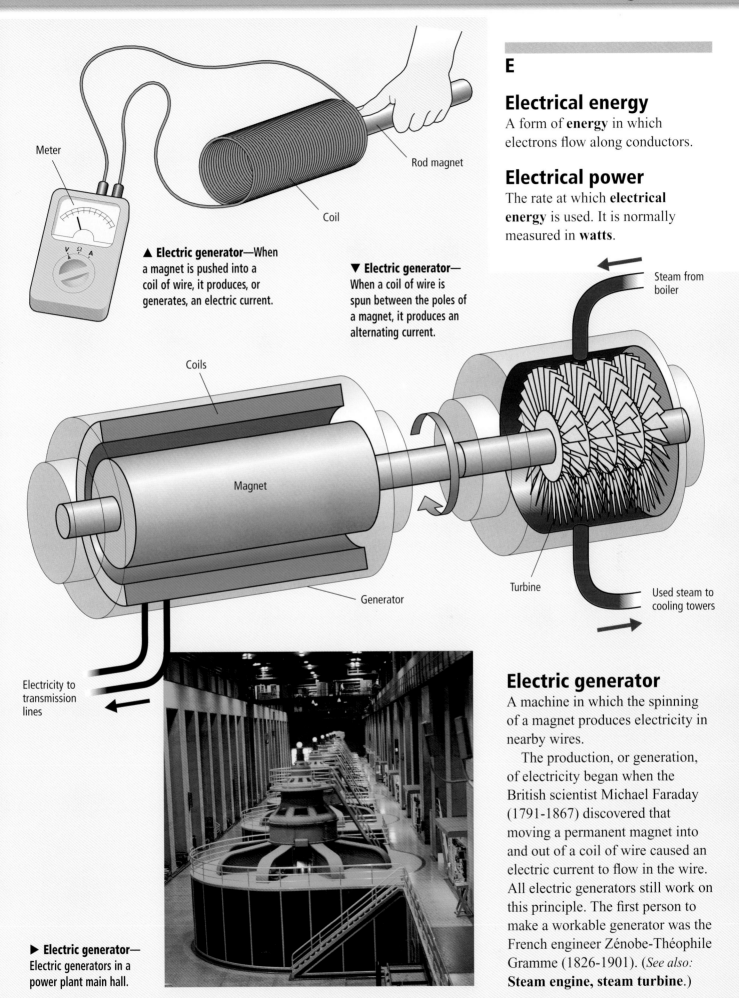

Meter

▲ Electric generator—When a magnet is pushed into a coil of wire, it produces, or generates, an electric current.

Rod magnet

Coil

▼ Electric generator—When a coil of wire is spun between the poles of a magnet, it produces an alternating current.

Coils

Magnet

Generator

Electricity to transmission lines

▶ Electric generator—Electric generators in a power plant main hall.

E

Electrical energy
A form of **energy** in which electrons flow along conductors.

Electrical power
The rate at which **electrical energy** is used. It is normally measured in **watts**.

Steam from boiler

Turbine

Used steam to cooling towers

Electric generator
A machine in which the spinning of a magnet produces electricity in nearby wires.

The production, or generation, of electricity began when the British scientist Michael Faraday (1791-1867) discovered that moving a permanent magnet into and out of a coil of wire caused an electric current to flow in the wire. All electric generators still work on this principle. The first person to make a workable generator was the French engineer Zénobe-Théophile Gramme (1826-1901). (*See also:* **Steam engine, steam turbine.**)

Electricity transmission

The way that electricity is carried from a **power plant** to the place where it is used, such as homes, businesses, or factories. Electricity is most efficiently transported using aluminum or copper wires. Wherever possible, they are hung from giant metal frames called pylons. The cables are not covered in insulating material because the air is a good insulator. In places where overhead transmission cables cannot be used, wires are run underground in protective sheaths. They may also need to be cooled by **oil**.

Electricity is sent along **transmission lines** at a very high voltage, usually several tens of thousands of volts, and sometimes hundreds of thousands of volts.

You can understand why such large voltages are important by looking at the way that voltage and current (amps) are related. This is shown as:

Watts (power) = volts x amps

A certain amount of **electrical power** can be sent with a low voltage and a high current, for example 100 watts = 2 volts x 50 amps; or at a high voltage and a small current, for example, 10 watts = 10 volts x 1 amp.

However, the more current that flows in a cable, the hotter it gets, and the more electricity is converted to **heat**. Thicker cables would be needed to transport more current, but they are more expensive and unwieldy. For these reasons electricity is transmitted along high-voltage lines rather than high-current lines. (*See also:* **Utility pole**.)

Electric light

(*See:* **Lamps and light energy**.)

▼ **Electricity transmission**—Electricity from a power plant is passed through a step-up transformer and converted to a very high voltage suited to long-distance transmission. The electricity is then stepped down for local distribution, often several times.

▶ **Electric motor**—Electric motors convert chemical energy to mechanical (kinetic) energy.

Electric motor

A machine that converts **electrical energy** into **mechanical energy** through the use of magnetism (magnetic energy). As electric current flows in a coil of wires, it produces a magnetic field. If this coil is placed on the shaft of a motor and surrounded by another magnet, the two magnets will influence one another, and the shaft will turn. Special devices (such as a collar called a commutator) are added to make sure that the motor continues to turn.

Electrochemical cell

More commonly known as a **battery**. Other names include Leclanché cell, for the French engineer Georges Leclanché (1839-1882); and the Daniell cell, for the British scientist John Daniell (1790-1845).

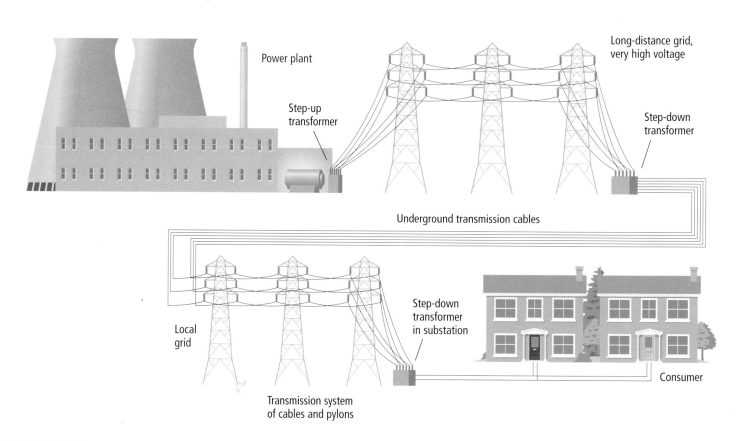

Power plant

Step-up transformer

Long-distance grid, very high voltage

Step-down transformer

Underground transmission cables

Local grid

Step-down transformer in substation

Consumer

Transmission system of cables and pylons

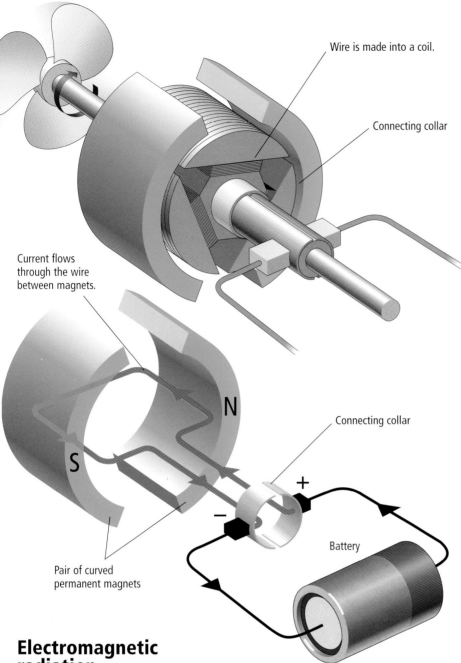

Wire is made into a coil.

Connecting collar

Current flows through the wire between magnets.

N

S

Connecting collar

+

−

Battery

Pair of curved permanent magnets

Electromagnetic radiation

Any form of **energy** that is sent as waves or rays between two places. It does not need a conductor, so this kind of energy can be sent through space. Radio waves, visible **light**, and x-rays are all forms of electromagnetic radiation.

The somewhat cumbersome term electromagnetic radiation is used because it was found that electricity and magnetism were both jointly responsible for many kinds of **radiation**. In space all electromagnetic energy moves at the same speed—299,792,458 meters per second.

Endothermic reaction

A chemical reaction that draws in **heat energy** from the surroundings. For example, when ammonium chloride is dissolved in water, the reaction causes the solution to become cold. (*Compare with:* **Exothermic reaction**.)

▶ **Endothermic reaction**—When barium hydroxide and ammonium nitrate are stirred together they take so much heat out of the surroundings that they cause water on the beaker to freeze. If the beaker is placed on a wet tile, the tile can easily be lifted up with the beaker—the two are frozen together by the ice.

Energy

The capacity for doing work. The word energy comes from the Greek *energeia*, meaning "activity."

Energy has many forms, for example, **potential**, **kinetic**, **light**, **heat**, **electrical**, **radiant**, **chemical**, elastic, **mechanical**, gravitational, mass, and **nuclear**. In some cases energy is connected with an object, for example, a ball held aloft or a tightly coiled spring, but in other cases it is not connected with matter, as for example, **light energy**. (This can be proved because light travels through a vacuum where there is no matter.)

Any form of energy is connected with movement. Even something at rest (like a coiled spring) has the capacity for causing movement. Chemicals in a **battery** have the capacity to make electrons flow in an electrical circuit. Energy can be converted from one form to another, although the total amount of energy remains the same (*see:* **Energy conversion**). (*See also:* **Calorie (Cal)**; **Conduction**; **Convection**; **Electromagnetic radiation**; **Energy supply**; **Entropy**; **Pollution**; **Radiation**.)

(*For other forms of energy see:* **Geothermal energy**; **Green energy**; **Hydroelectric power**; **Ocean energy**; **Photosynthesis**; **Renewable energy**; **Solar thermal energy**; **Sound energy**; **Tidal energy**; **Water power**; **Wind power**.)

Energy conversion

The change of **energy** from one form to another so that it can better serve human needs.

Energy cannot be created or destroyed; it can only be transformed, or converted, from one form to another. Because energy is so important to everything we do, people have developed many ways of converting natural sources of energy into forms that are most useful to their needs.

The earliest energy conversion occurred when people burned wood for fires (**fuel wood**), thereby changing **chemical energy** to **heat** and **light energy**. Some of the first mechanical devices for conversion were the windmill and the **waterwheel**. The **kinetic energy** of **wind** or flowing **water** was turned into **mechanical energy** for performing tasks like pumping water and grinding corn.

The mills were simple devices. Later, people discovered how to convert energy in more complex

▼ **Energy conversion**—Although energy can never be created or destroyed, when one form of energy is converted to another, low-level heat is always produced. Since we cannot use this heat, it is called an energy "loss."

This flow chart shows how heat is created at every step from the burning of fossil fuel in a power plant. The more conversion steps, the more energy is turned into heat, and the less there is available for the primary purpose of generating electicity.

ways using several steps. For example, **burning coal** (chemical energy) can be turned into heat energy, which can be used to produce **steam** (**potential energy**), which can then be released as a flow of steam (mechanical energy) to turn a **turbine** (mechanical energy), which then generates electricity (**electrical energy**), which lights a light bulb (light energy).

The problem with converting energy is that during each conversion, friction and air resistance turns energy into unwanted heat as well. This means that the conversion process is less efficient than it might ideally be. For example, the early steam engines made by James Watt, which converted heat energy from coal to mechanical energy, wasted 98% of the energy in the coal. They had an efficiency of just 2%. Even today, the highest energy efficiency of a **steam turbine** (the modern version of Watt's engine used to generate electricity in **power plants**) is just 40%. That is still far short of ideal. Car engines are even less efficient.

The most efficient converters should be those that change energy in just one step—for example, **solar cells** to turn sunshine into electricity. Many people are now

Energy supply

For society to function properly, the supply of large amounts of **energy** has to be managed successfully. Energy supply is therefore handled by a small number of very large companies or by national governments. **Electrical energy** and **natural gas** energy are provided through national grids of cables and pipes. **Gasoline** is supplied by a network of pipelines and tankers.

Entropy

The amount of **energy** that is unavailable for work. For example, before a log is burned, the amount of energy for work is high because all of the energy available is concentrated in the log. After it has burned, the energy is mostly in the form of **heat** scattered in the air. This heat energy is not available any more for useful work.

worried about the way that burning **fossil fuels** for energy is causing the **greenhouse effect** and air **pollution**. If the efficiency of burning and conversion could be improved, that would mean less pollution and less **global warming**.

(*For nature's process of energy conversion see:* **Photosynthesis**.)

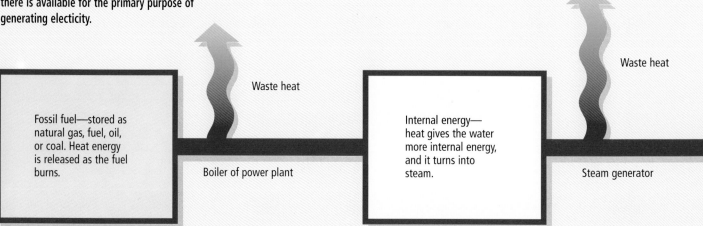

Fossil fuel—stored as natural gas, fuel, oil, or coal. Heat energy is released as the fuel burns.

Waste heat

Boiler of power plant

Internal energy—heat gives the water more internal energy, and it turns into steam.

Waste heat

Steam generator

Evaporation

The change of liquid to vapor below the **boiling point**, for example, when water disappears from a puddle. **Heat** for this process is taken from the surrounding air. Evaporation can therefore be used as a means of cooling, as in refrigeration.

Exothermic reaction

A reaction that gives out large amounts of **heat**. **Combustion**, for example, **burning** a log, is an example of an exothermic reaction. (*Compare with:* **Endothermic reaction**.)

Sulfuric acid

Sugar

▲ **Exothermic reaction**—Adding sulfuric acid to sugar produces the reaction shown above. The change to a black foam is accompanied by a great release of heat. This shows that sugar contains a large amount of stored energy that can be released as heat. The body makes use of such energy in a more controlled way.

Expansion

The increase in volume of an object when it is heated. The rate at which this occurs is called the coefficient of expansion. The coefficient of expansion of a gas is much greater than a liquid, which is, in turn, much greater than that of a solid. Metals tend to expand more than other solids.

The heat produced during the reaction drives off water as steam

Explosion

A violent form of **combustion**. There are two types of explosion. Extremely violent explosions are caused when a material decomposes very rapidly (as happens with a high explosive, such as TNT). This releases a large amount of **heat** and creates a shock wave from the **expansion** of the gases. The shock wave of a high explosive can be powerful enough to demolish buildings.

Ordinary explosions are a very rapid form of combustion. They produce a less intensive effect than a high explosive. Gunpowder is an example of an ordinary explosive.

F

Fat

A natural substance stored in the cells of plants and animals that is oily or greasy to the touch. There is no difference between oils and fats except that fats are solids at room temperature, while oils are liquids.

Living things store excess **energy** from their food as fat (*see:* **Food energy**). That is because fat contains twice the energy of any other kind of food weight for weight. Fat is therefore used as a storehouse of concentrated energy. It is particularly concentrated in seeds and near animal muscles. Some nuts are nearly three-quarters fat.

Waste heat

Movement energy— the steam turns the bladed wheel of a turbine.

Turbines

Electrical energy— the turbine generates electricity that is transmitted through cables.

Fission

A type of **nuclear** reaction in which the nucleus (center) of an atom splits into two smaller parts. Fission is not a common natural process on Earth, but is achieved artificially by bombarding the nucleus of a fissionable material, such as uranium, with high-speed nuclear particles, such as neutrons.

The amount of **energy** released from a fission reaction is extremely high. Fission is the process at work inside a nuclear reactor and nuclear bombs.

The first people to produce a fission reaction were Otto Hahn and Fritz Strassmann in 1938.

In a fission reaction neutrons are used to break up the nucleus of an atom because they have no electrical charge and so can easily break through the intense electrical field of the nucleus.

Fission is only possible with some atoms. Uranium-235 is the most common naturally occurring fissionable material. Other fissionable elements, such as plutonium-239, are made artificially as a result of the fission of uranium. (*See also:* **Fusion**.)

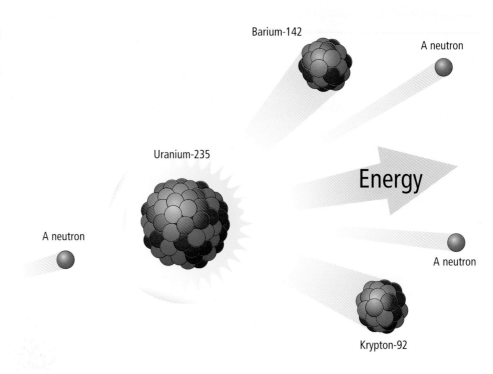

▲ **Fission**—The process that allows nuclear energy to be unlocked in power plants.

Flame

A mixture of two gases that react so fast that they give off **light** (and **heat**) **energy**. Usually, one of the gases is oxygen, and the other is a **fuel**. A flame will not occur when there is too little or too much fuel. A mixture of **natural gas** (fuel) and air, for example, will only burn if the proportion of natural gas is between 4% and 15%.

Flammable

Able to catch fire easily. Many flammable substances are liquids that vaporize easily, so that there is a mixture of vapor (which acts as a **fuel**) and oxygen available in the air.

Many flammable substances, such as the liquids and gases refined from **petroleum**, are carbon rich. For example, **kerosene** was burned in **lamps** for many years and is now used as an aircraft engine fuel; **gasoline** fuels motor vehicles.

Fluorescent lamp

A low-energy **lamp** that uses the property called fluorescence to produce light. Fluorescence is the release of **light** that occurs from some materials when they are exposed to **energy** from ultraviolet rays.

A fluorescent lamp consists of a glass tube filled with a vapor, usually mercury vapor. When an electric current flows through the vapor, it emits ultraviolet **radiation**. The inside of the tube is coated with phosphors. Phosphors are substances that fluoresce—change ultraviolet **radiation** into visible light.

Food energy

The **energy** contained in most kinds of food. Most food energy is concentrated in **fats** (as in avocados and meat), but energy is also found in sugars and starches (as in potatoes and cereals). Food energy is vital for all living things. Bodies contain supplies of very highly concentrated food energy, but these reserves will only last for a few days or weeks and must be regularly replaced by eating more food. (*See also:* **Carbohydrate** and **Chemical energy**.)

Fossil fuel

A **fuel** produced from plants or animals long ago that is found in the Earth's crust.

The main fossil fuels are **coal**, **lignite**, **natural gas**, and **crude oil** (**petroleum**). They were all formed from plants and animals buried tens or hundreds of millions of years ago. (*See also:* **Photosynthesis**.)

Fossil fuels are a concentrated form of **energy**. They will all burn in air to give out considerable amounts of **heat**. The heat can be used directly to keep warm. Alternatively, it can be used to turn water into **steam**, which in turn drives the **turbines** of electricity generators in **power plants**. It can also be used to heat a gas that expands, pushing a piston down. That is what happens inside an **internal combustion engine**.

Steam made from coal was used to power the machines and locomotives that created the Industrial Revolution. Fossil fuels now produce about nine-tenths of all the energy used by the main industrialized countries.

Fossil fuel reserves are limited. At the moment, new supplies are still being found, but in the future it is likely that petroleum will be the first to run out, with coal lasting the longest.

(*See also:* **Global warming; Greenhouse effect; Pollution**.)

Freezing point

The temperature at which a substance changes into a solid. It is the same temperature as the **melting point**. The freezing point of water is 0°C.

Fuel

Any material used to produce **heat** or **power** by **burning** (*see:* **Heat of combustion** and **Pyrolysis**). This includes **nuclear** material and food as well as **fossil fuels**, hydrogen, and wood (**fuel wood**). (*For individual fuels see:* **Charcoal; Coke; Diesel; Dung; Crude oil; Gasohol; Gasoline; Kerosene; Lignite; Liquefied natural gas (LNG); Liquefied petroleum gas (LPG); Methane; Natural gas; Peat; Petroleum**.)

Fuel cell

A device for converting **chemical energy** directly into electricity.

In principle a fuel cell is like an ordinary **battery**, having two electrodes bathed in a liquid called an electrolyte. However, a fuel cell can provide electricity for a much longer time than an ordinary battery. However, fuel cells are not simple devices like batteries. Fuel cells use gases that need to be pumped into the cell and special valves to control the amount of gases being pumped. The **fuel** in a fuel cell is often hydrogen gas, which has to be pumped into the fuel cell together with oxygen from an outside supply (*see:* **Hydrogen fuel**).

Fuel cells are very efficient at **converting energy** and so are used for generating electric **power** on spacecraft and other places where supplying fuel would be very difficult in any other way. The waste product of a fuel cell is water, and no polluting gases are given off.

▼ **Fossil fuel**—The main fossil fuels are coal, oil, and gas. This is the working face of a deep coal mine.

Fuel wood

Any wood that is used for heating, cooking, providing electric **power**, or powering **steam engines**. Most fuel wood is used in the developing world by people who cannot afford to buy **fossil fuels**. This kind of fuel wood runs small stoves that resemble camping stoves, so the majority of the wood required is in the form of sticks, not thicker trunks. Most people in the developing world use branches from trees as fuel wood.

In developing countries trees are often grown specially for fuel wood, with the leaves used to feed livestock. As the trees grow, the branches are periodically cut off, the leaves fed to livestock, and the branches used in fires.

In more developed countries wood is used in the form of chopped trunks and fed into wood-**burning** stoves and central heating systems. Fuel wood is often used because of its decorative effect, brightly burning in an open hearth. Some **power plants** burn fuel wood and sawdust.

▲ **Fuel wood**—It is a common source of energy in the developing world.

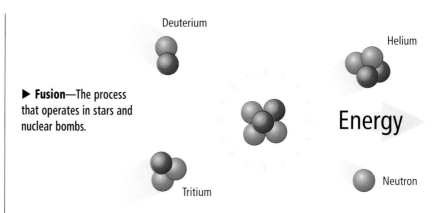

▶ **Fusion**—The process that operates in stars and nuclear bombs.

Deuterium

Tritium

Helium

Energy

Neutron

Fusion

A process that happens inside stars, such as the Sun, when the center of two atoms weld together. The result is a release of huge amounts of **energy**. The hydrogen bomb is an example of a small fusion reaction. However, it has not been possible so far to control the nature of fusion so that it can be used in **power plants**. (*Compare with:* **Fission**.)

G

Gasohol

A mixture of 90% unleaded **gasoline** and 10% ethanol (ethyl alcohol). Ethanol can be obtained from the grains of cereal plants and from potatoes. It is somewhat cheaper than gasoline and so becomes an attractive alternative as gasoline prices rise. Gasohol burns well in gasoline engines. Gasohol was pioneered on a large scale in countries like Brazil, which have no **petroleum** reserves of their own.

Gasoline

A mixture of hundreds of very light, **flammable** liquids that have been separated from **crude oil** by a heating process called cracking. Gasoline is also known simply as gas.

Gasoline is used as a **fuel** for **internal combustion engines**, such as those in motor vehicles. Gasoline gives out a great deal of **energy** as it burns. It is sprayed into the flow of air reaching an engine, and then compressed by a piston rising up a cylinder. It is then ignited with a spark from a spark plug, causing an **explosion** that forces the piston back down the cylinder.

Gasoline used to have lead added to improve **combustion**. However, the lead was a **pollution** hazard, and it is no longer added. That is why modern gasoline is called lead-free or unleaded. (*See also:* **Energy supply**.)

Geothermal energy

Any form of **energy** produced using **heat** from the Earth's interior. In most places it is impossible to reach the hot areas of the Earth because they are so far from the surface. However, under certain circumstances, such as when hot liquid rock called magma flows up into the crust (usually as the source of a volcano), the rocks near the surface become very hot.

The natural **power** of heated rocks is seen in the world's geysers, which shoot fountains of superheated water into the sky. Hot springs are also forms of geothermal energy. Geothermal heating has been used since Roman times. By tapping into sources of hot water, a supply can be piped into homes to provide **district heating**.

Geothermal energy becomes far more useful when it is converted into electricity, for this means that the energy can then be transported from where it occurs to places where it is needed.

Geothermal energy can be tapped when a supply of hot water is trapped underground. Because the water is under pressure, its temperature rises well above **boiling point** and becomes superheated. If a well is sunk down to the trapped water, and the superheated water is allowed to rise to the surface, the superheated water will "flash" into **steam**. The steam can be used to drive a **turbine** attached to an **electric generator**.

Not all hot rocks have natural supplies of water, but water can be fed down to them. Once the water has been superheated, it can be allowed to flow back to the surface and used as described above.

Because geothermal energy is nonpolluting, it is a **green** form of energy. Geothermal **power plants** are found in Italy, New Zealand, Japan, Iceland, Mexico, and the United States.

▲ **Geothermal energy**—The use of warm water from hot rocks for district heating by piping the water directly to homes. This geothermal generator is near Paris, France.

▼ **Geothermal energy**—When temperatures are high, water will flash into steam if brought to the surface quickly, and geothermal energy can be used to generate electricity in a way similar to all other steam turbine generating plants. This geothermal power plant is in California.

Global warming

The man-made rapid increase in the temperature of the Earth's atmosphere due to the **greenhouse effect**. It is a side effect of the use of large amounts of **fossil fuel**.

The rise in global air temperatures can have dramatic effects on both the air and the oceans. It is believed that as the air warms, the polar ice caps will melt more quickly, and that will in turn lead to a global rise in sea levels. Some small oceanic islands are already seeing a rise in sea level that is enough to swamp them.

The other main result of global warming is a rapid change in climatic belts. It is likely that the weather will get more unpredictable and stormy in some parts of the world, while becoming drier elsewhere. The result will be more disasters such as floods and droughts. Many species of wildlife will probably not be able to cope with the rapid changes brought about by global warming and will become extinct.

Global changes in the ocean are already noticeable in the form of the cycles of change called El Niño and La Niña. These cycles occur in the equatorial regions of the Pacific Ocean, producing a period of rapid warming and then cooling of parts of the ocean. That leads to great climatic change in places bordering the equator.

Glucose

A common form of the foodstuff we call sugar. Glucose is a simple sugar. It is found in fruits and honey, and is the most important free sugar carried in the bloodstream. It is a source of almost instant **energy** for the body.

Plants contain molecules of starch, each of which contains thousands of glucose units. Our bodies break down the starch when we eat, releasing the glucose and making it available as an energy supply for our bodies. It can also be artificially extracted and used as a high-energy food. Ordinary granulated sugar does not contain glucose. (*See also:* **Carbohydrate** and **Food energy**.)

Green energy

Any form of **energy** conversion that does not create **pollution**. Wind, water, and sunshine can all be thought of as "green" energy supplies. (*See also:* **Hydroelectric power**; **Geothermal energy**; **Renewable energy**; **Solar power**; **Solar thermal energy**; **Tidal energy**; **Water power**; **Waterwheels**; **Wind farms**; **Wind power**.)

Greenhouse effect

The **heat** retained by the Earth's atmosphere as a result of the gases it contains.

Sunshine mainly passes straight through the Earth's atmosphere without being absorbed by the gases in the air. As a result, much of the **radiation** is available to warm the oceans and the land.

The wavelength of radiation depends on the temperature of the body that is radiating. Because the Sun is very hot, it radiates at very short wavelengths. However, the land and sea are cool, so they radiate heat at much longer wavelengths. It is these long waves that are absorbed by gases in the air.

The main heat-absorbing gases are **carbon dioxide** (CO_2) and water vapor. By absorbing part of the radiation from the land and sea, these gases temporarily trap the heat in the atmosphere, making it much warmer than it would otherwise be. It is estimated that the Earth's atmosphere would be some 15°C colder without carbon dioxide and water vapor.

The amount of heat held by these gases depends on their concentration in the air. Although the amount of water vapor has not changed much over time, people have added considerably to the amount of carbon dioxide in the air by **burning fossil fuels**. As a result, the air is now able to hold more heat than a century or so ago.

(*See also:* **Global warming**.)

▼ **Greenhouse effect**—There are many ways of generating electricity, and only some release carbon dioxide (CO_2). However, they also happen to be the easiest and most developed technologies, which is why we use them. Most of the green technologies are still in an early stage of development.

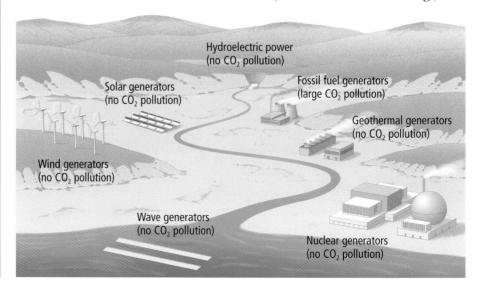

Hydroelectric power (no CO_2 pollution)

Solar generators (no CO_2 pollution)

Fossil fuel generators (large CO_2 pollution)

Geothermal generators (no CO_2 pollution)

Wind generators (no CO_2 pollution)

Wave generators (no CO_2 pollution)

Nuclear generators (no CO_2 pollution)

H

Heat

The form of **energy** that is involved when any kind of work is done. It is actually a form of **kinetic energy**. For example, heat is released when two sticks are rubbed together. Heat can also be produced by a chemical reaction. **Burning** wood in a fire, for example, is a chemical reaction that produces heat. Our bodies produce heat as they use chemical reactions to digest the food (**chemical energy**) we eat.

To understand that heat is continually on the move, just think about how hard we have to try to keep the heat inside our homes in the winter, or how hard we have to try to keep it out of our homes in the summer.

Raising the temperature of a substance adds energy and may cause a change. This change may be physical, such as a change in the volume, pressure, or density of the substance. For example, when a substance becomes warm, it usually swells. That is because the molecules it is made of now have more energy and move around more. When the **melting point** is reached, the energy of the molecules is so great they move further apart. Increasing the temperature of a liquid sufficiently causes the molecules to separate completely, and the liquid then changes into gas (*see:* **Heat of vaporization**).

The change that occurs may also be chemical. For example, a very high temperature can break down a compound—heat causes **coal** to break down into carbon, oxygen, water vapor, and **carbon dioxide** gases.

Heat is moved from one object to another because they are at

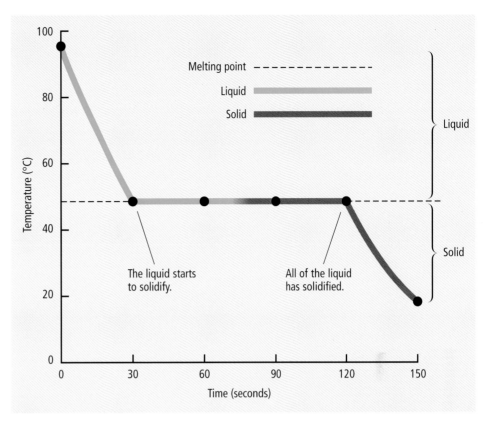

▲ **Heat**—When a liquid is cooled, a state is reached at which heat continues to be lost, but the temperature stays the same. This happens at the freezing point. It demonstrates that heat and temperature are not the same.

different temperatures. Heat flows from the hotter object to the cooler. That is because the molecules in the hotter material are moving more vigorously than in the cooler material, and as they bump into the surface molecules of the cooler material, they pass on more energy than they receive back (*see:* **Convection**).

Although heat is often connected with a change in temperature, the two are not the same. Heat is a form of energy. That is different from temperature, which is a measure of the amount of heat energy in an object. You can see this when heat energy is used to change liquid water to **steam** at its **boiling point**. The temperature does not change, but heat energy has to be added to cause the **change of state**. (*See also:* **Latent heat**.)

Heat energy is measured in **joules**, **calories**, and BTUs. The joule is the "scientific" measure of all forms of energy (including heat energy). One joule is one **watt** second. The calorie (a more traditional term and replaced in scientific circles in 1948) is the amount of heat needed to raise the temperature of one gram of water from 14.5°C to 15.5°C. A calorie is 4.2 joules.

The British Thermal Unit (BTU), still widely used in the United States, is the amount of energy needed to raise the temperature of one pound of water from 63°F to 64°F.

One BTU is approximately 252 calories or 1,058 joules.

The heat energy in food is a different kind of calorie, known as the **kilocalorie**. It is equal to 1,000 calories. (*See also:* **Heat capacity; Heat conservation; Heat transfer**.)

Heat capacity

The amount of **energy** needed to raise a kilogram of a substance 1°C. Materials can absorb different amounts of **heat**. Heat capacity is also known as the specific heat of the substance.

Chemists have found that the heat capacity of an element is quite closely related to its atomic weight. In general, the heavier the element, the more heat it absorbs before its temperature rises 1°C. Water has an unusually high heat capacity in this respect.

Heat conservation

Saving heat. The home is the focus of many kinds of **energy** use and energy transfer. They are shown in the diagram below. Usually the main concern of people is to reduce their energy costs. That can be done in part by choosing between **fuel** sources and supplying companies, but is mostly achieved through energy-**conservation** measures.

▼ **Heat conservation—**The way heat is lost in the home and how to conserve as much heat as possible.

Heat exchanger

A piece of machinery developed to allow **heat** to be moved between hot and cold fluids without them coming into contact. In this case a fluid is either a gas or a liquid.

The cooling system of a car uses a heat exchanger in the form of the radiator in the front of the car. Hot liquid circulates around the engine and takes heat from the cylinders into the radiator. The radiator has many fins, which can then effectively transfer heat to the air.

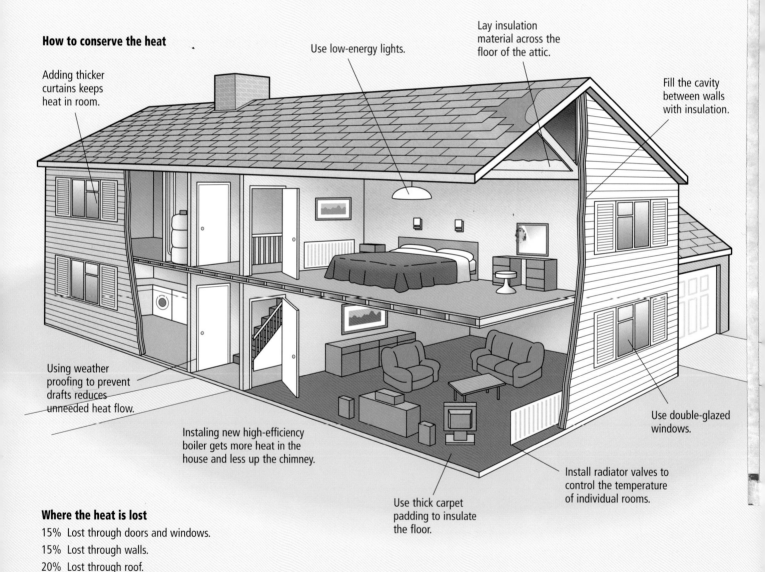

How to conserve the heat

Adding thicker curtains keeps heat in room.

Use low-energy lights.

Lay insulation material across the floor of the attic.

Fill the cavity between walls with insulation.

Using weather proofing to prevent drafts reduces unneeded heat flow.

Installing new high-efficiency boiler gets more heat in the house and less up the chimney.

Use thick carpet padding to insulate the floor.

Use double-glazed windows.

Install radiator valves to control the temperature of individual rooms.

Where the heat is lost

15% Lost through doors and windows.

15% Lost through walls.

20% Lost through roof.

30% Lost through drafty window frames, badly fitting doors, and necessary ventilation.

10% Lost through the floor.

Note: These figures are a guide to energy loss. The actual values will vary depending on the house, its physical setting in the landscape, and local costs of buying and adding the features.

Another heat exchanger works in air-conditioning systems and in refrigerators, where the **expansion** of a gas in pipes makes them cool. The air surrounding the pipes is also cooled, thereby cooling down the inside of the house or refrigerator.

Heat exchangers also work in home hot water and central heating systems. A fire in a boiler heats the water used to run the central heating system. A set of pipes carries the hot water to the taps.

In industry heat exchangers can be of enormous size. One very easily spotted heat exchanger is the cooling tower of a **power plant**.

This concrete column may be tens, even a hundred meters high and works like a giant car radiator. Inside, the hot water brought from the power plant is allowed to spill down a grating. As it does so, it is cooled by the cold air that flows through the tower. A little of the water is lost as **steam**, but most drips down to the bottom of the tower, where it can be collected and pumped back to cool the power plant **turbines** once more.

▼ **Heat exchanger**—Cooling towers at a power plant are one of the most dramatic examples of a heat exchanger.

Heat of combustion

The **heat** given out when a **fuel** is burned. It gives an indication of how much heat **energy** is concentrated in the fuel.

Heat of vaporization

The amount of **heat** needed to change a liquid to a vapor (**vaporization**) at its **boiling point**. For example, one gram of water needs 540 **calories** of heat to turn it to vapor (or in chemical units, 40.65 **kilojoules** per mole).

Heat transfer

Heat can be transferred in three ways: by **conduction**, by **convection**, and by **radiation**.

Conduction occurs when two objects touch. Heat can then flow from one object to another. Conduction can occur in solids, liquids, and gases.

Convection is the transfer of heat by the movement of particles within a gas or liquid. It cannot occur in a solid.

Convection relies on the fact that warm liquids and gases rise. For example, if a pan of cold water is placed on a stove, the heat is transferred by conduction from the pan to the bottom of the liquid. The liquid then warms up and becomes less dense than the cooler water above. As a result, it rises up to the surface. As the warm water rises, cold water sinks to take its place and is warmed in turn. Convection is this circulation of liquid or gas. The heating source must be from below.

Radiation is the transfer of **energy** from one place to another without anything in between. The Sun shares its heat with the Earth by radiation. The heat from the Sun travels 150 million km through space to reach the Earth.

(*See also:* **Insulation**.)

Hydroelectric power

The **electrical energy** produced by converting the **energy** of water.

The energy of flowing water can be seen all around us. It is most spectacularly shown at waterfalls, where the water is falling from a height. It is the combination of the volume of water and the speed of flow that gives the waterfall its extra energy.

The energy in water can be converted to electrical energy by forcing the water to flow through a **turbine**—a type of propeller attached to the shaft of an **electric generator**.

The energy of flowing water depends on the amount of water and the speed it is flowing.

The energy of flowing water is equal to ½ (mv^2), where m is the mass of the liquid, and v its velocity. Thus a large river flowing at a moderate speed may produce the same energy as a much smaller river tumbling down a mountainside. Obviously, a combination of a large river and high speed produces the largest amount of energy.

Hydroelectric **power** is a "green" form of energy—it is friendly to the environment insofar as it does not release any **polluting** gases into the air in the way that **burning fossil fuels** does.

In the case of large rivers only a small fall (called "head") of water may be needed to generate large amounts of electricity. Many hydroelectric **power plants** can simply be placed in the weirs next to navigation locks on rivers. The Rhine in Germany and the Ohio River in North America are two examples. Some hydroelectric plants can be placed where there is a natural head of water, such as next to a waterfall. Some of the water that would have gone over the falls is then diverted

through **turbines**. The hydroelectric power plants at Niagara on the United States-Canada border are of this type.

However, large hydroelectric plants need a large, reliable amount of water, which cannot be supplied from rivers whose flow changes seasonally. To guarantee the supply, water has to be stored by building

dams and creating reservoirs. Wherever possible, dam sites are chosen where rivers flow in deep valleys. This reduces the cost of building a dam and also cuts the loss of water by **evaporation** from the reservoir surface in summer. Nevertheless, reservoirs may flood large areas of fertile land or precious wilderness, and in this

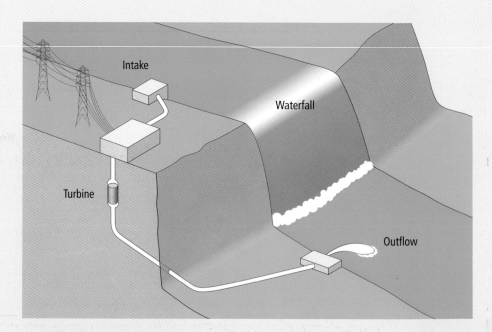

▲▼ **Hydroelectric power**—There are two main ways of getting hydroelectric power: by using a large head of water, as for example, by diverting some water from a waterfall (top), or building a tall dam or a large barrage across a major river (bottom).

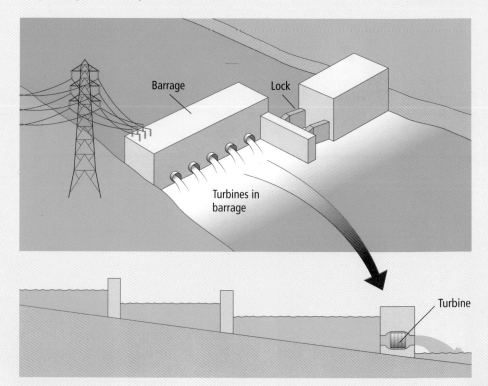

way most hydroelectric energy has an environmental cost.

Creating a reservoir also increases the height of the water level and allows water to flow faster through a turbine. The great dams and reservoirs on the Colorado River in the southwestern United States (for example, Boulder Dam and Lake Mead) are examples.

(*See also:* **Pumped storage**.)

▶▼ **Hydroelectric power**—The hydroelectric power plant (right) at Niagara Falls (below) is a waterfall diversion.

▼ **Hydroelectric power**—Hoover power plant creates a large head of water by using a tall dam.

▼ **Hydroelectric power**—The hydroelectric power plant on the Ohio River uses a barrage.

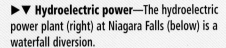

Hydrogen fuel

Hydrogen can be used as a **fuel** in a **fuel cell**. Fuel cells work by combining hydrogen and oxygen in a special kind of **battery**.

Hydrogen can also be used as fuel in space vehicles. In this case hydrogen and oxygen are also used, but they are burned in a **combustion** chamber. The large **expansion** of gases that results is directed through nozzles and can propel a rocket out of the Earth's gravity.

▼ **Hydrogen fuel**—The rockets that launch the Space Shuttle use hydrogen as a fuel.

I

Insulation

A material designed to slow down the flow of **heat energy**.

Insulators have to stop the three means of **heat transfer**: **conduction**, **convection**, and **radiation**. To achieve this, a combination of materials is often required.

Because all metals are good conductors of heat, nonconducting insulation is made of nonmetallic materials. Thermal insulating materials include fiberglass, polystyrene foam, and cork. One of the best thermal insulators is air. Air has the further attraction of being free. However, because air is a gas, it will readily circulate by the process of convection. If allowed to convect, air will carry heat around—the reverse of what is intended for an insulator. To prevent air circulating, and to use its insulating qualities, air is trapped in small pockets or bubbles inside other materials. This can be seen in the way that woollen clothing works. The main insulation is not the wool, but the air trapped between the fibers. As a result, a coarse wool woven to make a coarsely knitted sweater will be much warmer than the same wool woven into a fine yarn and knitted to a smooth finish. For the same reason several layers of thin clothing are warmer than a single layer of thick clothing.

In attic and wall insulation polystyrene foam is often used. Here the air is trapped in the polystyrene as evenly spaced bubbles. In fiberglass the air is trapped between the fibers in the same way as wool. Glass is also a good insulator.

Radiation can be stopped by reflecting the radiated heat. Metals are good reflectors and are used on the surfaces of poor conductors. A silver coating is often used on the inside of thermos flasks to prevent radiation loss from a hot liquid. An aluminum sheet is sometimes stuck to the surface of wallboards and ceiling boards to reflect heat back into the room and prevent it from being lost through the walls.

▼ **Insulation**—Old houses can have their insulation improved by using a combination of thermal bricks, aluminum foil, and insulating fiber.

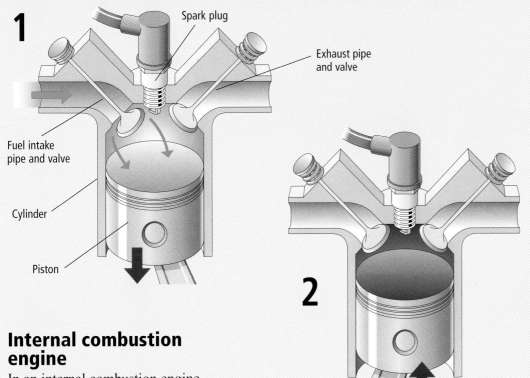

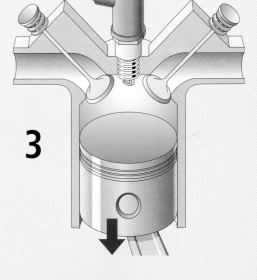

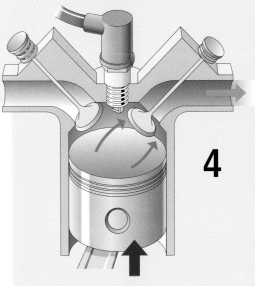

Internal combustion engine

In an internal combustion engine, such as a car engine, a **fuel** and oxygen from the air are burned together inside the engine. When this happens, the products of the **combustion** expand, and they push a piston down a cylinder. This movement can be used in many ways, such as generating electricity as well as powering cars.

In an external combustion engine the combustion occurs outside the engine. For example, in a **steam engine** the **steam** is produced outside the engine when fuel is burned to **heat** water and produce the steam in a boiler.

An internal combustion engine is more efficient than an external combustion engine and can be made more compact and portable.

That is why **gasoline** engines began to replace steam engines at the end of the 19th century.

The first internal combustion engine was built by Nikolaus August Otto (1832-1891) and burned **coal** powder. In 1885 it was modified to burn gasoline by Gottlieb Daimler (1834-1900).

The **diesel** engine is even more efficient than the gasoline engine. The diesel has slower acceleration than the gasoline engine because it takes more time to build up **power**. That is why it is preferred for trucks rather than cars.

J

Joule (J)

The unit of **heat energy**. It was named after James Prescott Joule (1818-1889), who showed that the heat produced is directly proportional to the work done (energy put in). In other words, heat is simply a form of energy. The unit of heat energy, the joule, is a very small amount, and most practical applications of the joule use the **kilojoule (kJ)**.

One calorie is equal to 4.2 joules.

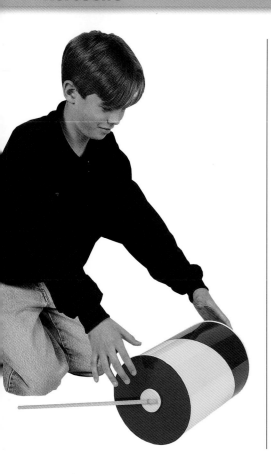

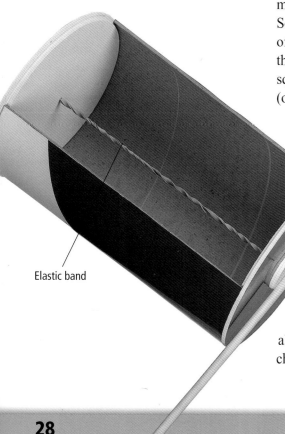

▲▼ **Kinetic energy**—The principle of kinetic energy can be seen in this model. It contains a rubber band that is wound up to make extra potential energy. When the model is released, the rubber band unwinds and converts potential energy into kinetic energy. As a result, the model moves forward. The same principle is used on model aircraft.

Elastic band

K

Kerosene

Also known as paraffin, kerosene is one of the products of **petroleum** distillation. Kerosene is a heavier **fuel** than **gasoline**. It was widely used for lighting in the days before gas and electric lighting. It is now an aircraft fuel. (*See also:* **Flammable** and **Lamps and light energy**.)

Kilocalorie

One thousand **calories**. The unit often used for measuring the **energy** in food.

Kilojoule (Kj)

One thousand **joules**. The common unit of **heat energy**.

Kinetic energy

The **energy** of movement. Kinetic energy is a combination of speed and mass. A large ball moving quickly through the air will have a greater kinetic energy than the same ball moving slowly or a ball made from a less dense material. Scientists calculate the amount of kinetic energy (ke) as half of the mass (m) multiplied by the square of the speed (velocity, v) (or $ke = \frac{1}{2} mv^2$).

Kinetic energy is measured in **joules**. A two-kilogram ball moving at a speed of one meter per second has a kinetic energy of one joule.

Kinetic energy is changed to **heat** energy when, for example, a ball flies through the air and is slowed down by air resistance. When the ball stops, all of the kinetic energy has been changed to heat energy.

Kinetic energy changes to potential (position) energy when a ball moves up a slope. When it comes to rest at the top of a slope, the ball has no more kinetic energy—it has all been changed into **potential energy**. When the ball rolls back down the slope, the potential energy is changed back into kinetic energy again. (*See also:* **Mechanical energy**.)

L

Lamps and light energy

A lamp is something that produces **light**. Light **energy** was first produced from **chemical energy** using a wick soaked in **fat**. The earliest lamps were hollowed-out rocks and shells. Later the containers were made of pottery.

Torches, made of bundles of sticks whose ends were dipped in fat and ignited, made more light than wick lamps.

Latent heat

The amount of **energy** needed to make a substance have a **change of state** from liquid to solid or gas. Latent heat is not the amount of **heat** but simply vibration of molecules within the substance. For example, boiling can take place in a microwave without any external source of heat.

Light

A form of **radiation energy**. People normally use the word light to mean the kind of radiation that can be seen by the human eye (also called visible light).

◄▲ **Lamps and light energy**—Light energy is mainly obtained by converting fuels either to make electricity (as in the case of the bulb above right) or for direct burning such as in a flame. Flames (as the gas jet above) give out light because of the incandescence produced by the tiny carbon particles created when a fuel burns in air. However, as the candle (left) shows, a flame is relatively poor at giving out light. As a result, nearly all modern lighting is by electricity.

The development of lamps made remarkably little progress for thousands of years, and lamps used in medieval times were no better than those used by the ancient Greeks.

The first major improvement in lamp design was made in the 18th century when the wick was placed in a metal tube and its height controlled by a thumbscrew. That allowed a variable amount of light. At the same time, it was discovered that the light could be improved by drawing more air past the **burning** wick so that **combustion** became more effective. As a result, a chimney was added to the lamp.

The original **fuels** used in lamps were olive oil, tallow, beeswax, fish oil, and whale oil. In the middle of the 19th century they were replaced by distilled **petroleum** oil called **kerosene** or paraffin.

Lamps using gas were invented at the end of the 18th century.

The gas came from burning **coal** and was called coal gas. Gas was soon used for street lighting and for those households that could afford to install gas pipes. It produced a far better light output than oil lamps.

All of these lamps produced a yellow light—from the **flame**. But a new kind of burner was then made for the gas lamp, consisting of a cotton net, called a mantle. When gas and air were introduced to the inside of the mantle, and the mantle was lighted, it glowed with an intense white light. This form of light is still used for gas camping lights. Electric light began as incandescent lamps— light is produced when the flow of electricity through a wire makes it so hot it gives off light. Electric light was developed only at the end of the19th century due to the difficulty of making a filament in a light bulb that would last more than a few hours. Today these incandescent lights are the main form of lighting, together with **fluorescent** and vapor lamps.

Lignite

Also known as **brown coal**, lignite is a soft form of **coal** made from peat. It still has some of the fibers left from the **peat**, but has been compressed and changed so that it has a far higher **heat** value than peat. It is the first stage on the way to black coal formation. Lignite is about two-thirds to three-quarters carbon, as opposed to black coal, which is over 90% carbon.

Lignite is found very extensively in beds up to 30m thick. It may make up nearly half of all the world's known reserves of coal. However, because it is much more bulky than coal and can catch fire spontaneously if left out in the open, it has been used only in places where it is possible to burn it close to where it is extracted. This means that large reserves have so far been left completely undeveloped.

Lignite is normally mined by open-pit methods using huge bucket-wheel excavators. The lignite is soft and is scooped up by the buckets and dumped onto conveyor belts. The lignite is carried directly to **power plants** located nearby.

Liquefied natural gas (LNG)

Natural gas (which is mainly **methane**) that has been cooled below its **boiling point** of -162°C so that it turns from a gas into a liquid. Liquids occupy much less volume than gases, so liquefying the gas makes it easier to transport.

Liquefying natural gas has made it easier to use natural gas from wells that would be uneconomical to reach by pipeline. It also allows natural gas to be transported between continents using specially constructed tankers.

▲ **Lignite**—Lignite occurs in thick seams, often at shallow depth. The fuel is mined in huge pits like this one in Germany.

Liquefied petroleum gas (LPG)

A mixture of propylene, propane, butylene, and butane gases. It has been used as a portable source of **fuel** since the early days of **crude oil** distillation in the 1860s. These gases are all odorless, so a chemical called mercaptan is added to provide a warning smell in case of leaks.

LPG is obtained from **natural gas**. Natural gas normally also contains heavy **petroleum** compounds that have to be removed for efficient burning. The petroleum gas is then liquefied by cooling it below its **boiling point**. This reduces its volume and makes it easier to transport in cylinders. It is used for domestic heating. Camping gas is normally butane or a similar gas, not LPG.

M

Mechanical energy

The combined **energy** of movement (**kinetic energy**) and position (**potential energy**).

A pendulum that is stationary at the top of its swing has no kinetic energy because it is still. Ignoring friction and air resistance, as the pendulum goes down to the bottom of its swing, it loses potential energy and gains kinetic energy.

At the bottom of the swing the pendulum has only kinetic energy and no potential energy. However, all of the time, and no matter where on the swing it is, the total energy of the pendulum remains the same. That is its mechanical energy.

Mechanical energy is conserved if an object moves without any effects of friction. Mechanical energy is almost conserved for the Moon orbiting the Earth because there is no air in space to cause friction. The Moon makes an oval orbit; and when it is farthest from the Earth, its speed is slowest. It then speeds up as it gets closer to the Earth and then slows down again. This is similar to the pendulum. (The difference in speed is, however, not noticeable!)

Melting point

The temperature at which a solid changes into a liquid. It is the same temperature as the **freezing point**. The melting point of water is 0°C.

Methane

A colorless and odorless gas that is produced during the decomposing of organic material in an environment with limited oxygen, such as when the remains of living tissues decompose when buried in rocks.

Methane can be used as a **fuel**. It is the main component of **natural gas**, which forms deep inside rocks. It is also found naturally in **coal** mines and in swamps, where it is often called marsh gas. Methane is also created in sewage plants and garbage dumps as the organic matter decomposes.

Methane can be extracted from natural gas or by distilling coal, when it is known as coal gas or town gas.

Methane and natural gas are effectively the same.

N

Natural gas

A colorless and odorless gas produced deep within rocks as a result of the natural decomposition of ancient organisms. Natural gas is formed over many millions of years and so is called a **fossil fuel**.

Natural gas is one of the forms of **petroleum** and is often found together with the other constituent of petroleum, **crude oil**.

Natural gas is up to 90% **methane**, with smaller amounts of other gases such as ethane, propane, and butane.

Natural gas forms as buried organisms decay. If the decay happens in a rock with connecting pores, such as sandstone, then the gas can move through the rock. Under special conditions the gas can be trapped within the rock.

That happens if the rock above where the gas is forming is a gas-tight type of rock such as shale.

Natural gas can become concentrated if the shape of the rock formations is favorable, for example, if the rocks are folded up into a dome. The gas will then build up in the rocks close to the top of the dome.

When natural gas occurs in large amounts, it is worth exploiting. A region of exploitable natural gas is called a gas field.

Natural gas is obtained by sinking a well. When the well reaches the gas, the gas usually flows up the well of its own accord because it naturally occurs under great pressure within the rocks. (*See also:* **Oil rig**.)

Most natural gas is a mixture of many gases. Some of the gases, such as sulfur dioxide and hydrogen sulfide, are undesirable, even in trace amounts, when the natural gas is used for heating or cooking. They are removed before the gas is distributed. At the same time, gases such as butane and propane that can be used more profitably are also removed as **liquefied petroleum gas (LPG)**.

Because methane is odorless, a small amount of a chemical is added to give the gas a smell. This is done for safety reasons—to warn of leaks.

When natural gas is cooled and made into a liquid, it fills a space only one six-hundredth of the size it was as a gas. **Liquefied natural gas (LNG)** can be transported profitably in special tankers.

Natural gas has become one of the most important **fuels** in industrialized countries. It began to replace **coal**, or town, gas in the 1930s and had totally replaced coal gas by the 1960s. Its main use now is as a heating fuel and as a fuel for electricity-generating plants. Natural gas is transported from gas fields to homes and factories by extensive pipeline networks and ships.

▲ **Natural gas**—Natural gas is obtained from petroleum fields. This is a gas plant near Midland, Texas.

Noncombustible

A material that will not combust (*see:* **Combustion**).

Nuclear energy

The **energy** that is released when the centers, or nuclei, of atoms are split apart. Nuclear reactions are called **fission** reactions and referred to as "splitting the atom." Nuclear energy is also known as atomic energy.

The fission reactions that are needed to release nuclear energy are difficult to make happen in a controlled way. They occur in special structures called nuclear reactors. They are carefully constructed to contain the radiation involved. The most common nuclear material is uranium-235. The fission process creates **heat** that is then used to create **steam** and drive **turbines** in the same way as more traditional **power plants**.

Nuclear energy was a popular energy source among countries that had very little reserves of **fossil fuels**. Countries like Japan and France still get most of their electricity from nuclear reactors. In many other industrial countries, over one-fifth of the total energy consumption is electricity, making nuclear energy a very important energy source.

Due to difficulties caused by poor construction techniques, especially in eastern Europe, and the resulting nuclear accidents, the number of new reactors being built has declined dramatically. There have also been accidents in western reactors, though they have always been on a containable scale.

Nuclear energy has the environmental bonus of not creating any greenhouse gases, unlike fossil fuels. On the down side, nuclear waste is radioactive, difficult to deal with, and remains hazardous for many centuries after use.

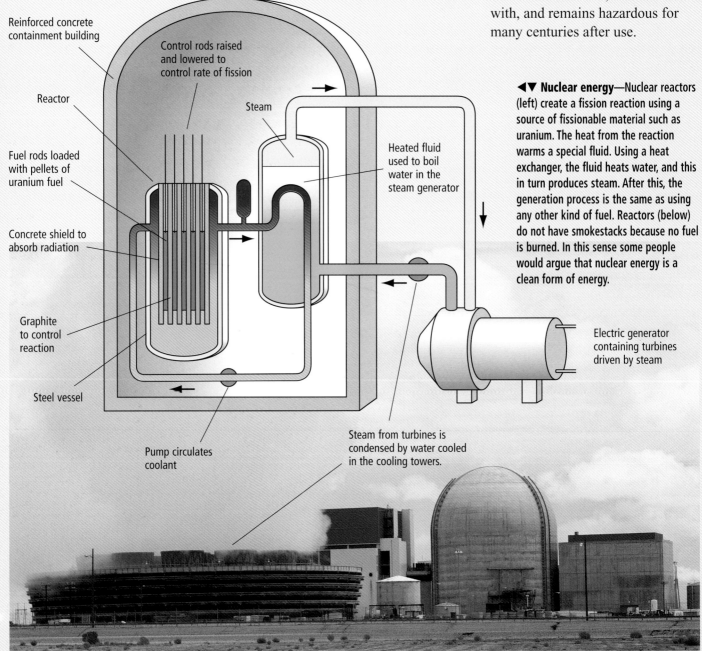

Reinforced concrete containment building

Control rods raised and lowered to control rate of fission

Reactor

Steam

Fuel rods loaded with pellets of uranium fuel

Heated fluid used to boil water in the steam generator

Concrete shield to absorb radiation

Graphite to control reaction

Steel vessel

Pump circulates coolant

Steam from turbines is condensed by water cooled in the cooling towers.

Electric generator containing turbines driven by steam

◄▼ **Nuclear energy**—Nuclear reactors (left) create a fission reaction using a source of fissionable material such as uranium. The heat from the reaction warms a special fluid. Using a heat exchanger, the fluid heats water, and this in turn produces steam. After this, the generation process is the same as using any other kind of fuel. Reactors (below) do not have smokestacks because no fuel is burned. In this sense some people would argue that nuclear energy is a clean form of energy.

O

Ocean energy

The world's oceans are vast bodies of moving water. The movement (**kinetic**) **energy** in them is immense. The problems come in harnessing the energy because it is not in a concentrated form.

The main ways in which the energy of ocean waters (as opposed to the winds that blow over them) can be used are through the changing tides (known as **tidal power** generation), the difference between warm and cold parts of the oceans (known as ocean thermal energy), and the harnessing of moving waves (direct wave energy).

The funnel shape of some estuaries causes water to be driven inland during each rising tide (flood tide). This raises the level of water in the estuary by many meters. On the falling (ebb) tide the water surges back out again. Tidal power generation harnesses this energy by building a barrage across the estuary and then forcing the water to flow in and out of the estuary through **turbines**. The best known of such **power plants** is on the Rance River in western France. It generates 240 megawatts of power.

However, tidal power is destined to remain a very minor source of ocean energy because the physical locations where it can be employed are very restricted, and at those places where it can be achieved, such as Penobscot Bay, Maine, or the Severn Estuary, England, there is great concern about the environmental damage that would be caused should the bays be enclosed.

In the tropics the surface waters are very warm, soaking up **solar radiation** equivalent in **heat** content to **burning** about 170 billion barrels of **oil** each day. However, all of this heat is soaked up only at the surface. The deep waters remain very cold. Ocean thermal conversion works something like a refrigerator—the expanding gases in the system turn a turbine that generates electricity. At present such generators produce only a very small amount of energy.

Oil

Short for **crude oil**, a form of **petroleum**.

Oil rig

A tower designed to hold the equipment needed for drilling and recovering **crude oil** or **natural gas**. It normally contains a pyramid of scaffolding called a derrick. The pipes and drilling equipment are hung from the derrick.

P

Peat

A fibrous, spongy material made from plant remains that decayed in swamps, bogs, and marshes. In these places the vegetation does not fully rot; so, as new plants form on the old, the remains of earlier plants are simply packed down under the new.

The weight of new plant matter gradually compresses the old remains and squeezes out some water, but peat remains soft and wet.

Peat is a source of **energy**, but it is not as concentrated as **lignite** or black **coal**. Peat has to be dried before it can be burned. Then it burns with a smoky **flame**. Its use is limited to traditional home heating.

▼ **Oil rig**—This is an oil rig in the North Sea.

Petroleum

Technically, a mixture of thousands of carbon-based substances, called hydrocarbons, that are produced in the Earth as a result of the decay of plant (*see:* **Photosynthesis**) and animal life. Petroleum contains both gases and liquids. The gases are called **natural gas**, and the liquids are called **crude oil**, or just **oil**. In more common usage the word petroleum is used to mean just crude oil. Petroleum is the most important of the world's **fossil fuels**.

The first knowledge of petroleum came when people saw a thick black liquid seeping from rocks. This thick part of petroleum is called bitumen. The more easily **evaporated** parts of the crude oil and natural gas were rarely seen (unless they seeped out in natural pools) because they evaporated as soon as they reached the surface.

To make use of crude oil, it had to be processed before it seeped out to the surface. Processing produced a form of lighter oil called **kerosene** (paraffin) that was first used instead of animal oil in **lamps**. The first well for this use was drilled by E. L. Drake at Titusville, Pennsylvania, in 1859. It was so successful that many more wells sprang up all over the United States and in other countries, too.

At first, small, shallow wells were enough to meet the need for lamps. At this time the automobile had not been invented, and no one thought of using oil for heating.

The invention of the **internal combustion engine** and its use in automobiles added greatly to the demand for crude oil. One part of crude oil, known as **gasoline**, was ideal for such engines. The remaining parts were at first discarded but were later used for heating and making chemicals.

It was also discovered that petroleum, either as refined oil or natural gas, could be used in **power plants** to generate electricity. Today, petroleum in its various forms provides nearly two-thirds of the **energy** needs of the world.

As demand grew, exploration followed. The world's greatest supplies of petroleum were found to be in the Middle East, but substantial supplies also existed in North America, in the Caribbean Sea, the North Sea, Russia, and parts of Africa.

It took hundreds of millions of years for oil to form, and special geological conditions are necessary for it to be trapped. These conditions are not commonly found. The decaying plants and animals had to be trapped in a rock with spaces (pores) in it that allowed the petroleum to move once it had been created. Petroleum

▶ **Petroleum**—The various parts, or fractions, of petroleum are shown here in proportion to the quantities obtained.

▼ **Petroleum**—A petroleum refinery.

Gases are collected for making other products and for producing heat.

Gasoline is the main fuel for automobiles.

Trucks and railroad engines use diesel oil.

About half the crude oil is made of heavy fuel oil. It can be used to run power plants and the engines of ships, but it cannot be used for automobiles.

Photosynthesis

The natural process of **energy conversion** using sunlight that occurs in most plants. The word photosynthesis means "putting together with **light**." Sunlight is captured by green-colored pigments in plant cells and converted to **chemical energy**. The light energy is used to change water, **carbon dioxide**, and minerals in the plant into oxygen and energy-rich substances called **carbohydrates**. Carbohydrates are sources of chemical energy. Some carbohydrates called sugars (such as the **glucose** in energy drinks) release their energy quickly, while others called starches (foods like potatoes, rice, and cereals) release their energy more slowly.

Photosynthesis is the most important energy-converting process on Earth. Without it plants could not grow, and animals (which depend on plants for their food) could not live. At the same time, this form of energy conversion releases oxygen that is needed for animals to breathe.

Photosynthesis is also the origin of **fossil fuels** such as **coal** and **natural gas**. They are simply the compressed and decayed remains of plant and animal tissues.

Photosynthesis is still the basic energy source for all animal life, and its results are directly or indirectly contained in the food we eat.

is less dense than water, and so it would slowly seep upward through water. Above the porous rock there had to be a gas and liquid-tight rock to keep the petroleum from escaping once it had formed. Given all of these conditions, pockets of trapped gas and oil could form.

Of the known petroleum fields, it is thought that about one-third of the world's oil reserves have been used already, and somewhat less than one-fifth of the natural gas. At current rates of use these reserves have less than a century left before they are gone completely. It is for this reason that so much effort is going into finding alternative fuels. However, it is by no means certain that all reserves have been found.

Natural gas and crude oil separate naturally. Crude oil is heated to separate the mixture of substances it contains. Each of the liquids has a different **boiling point** and will boil off separately, after which the vapor can be cooled. This process is called distillation, and the place where it happens is called a **refinery**.

Pollution

The presence in the environment of substances that cause harm. **Energy** production is one of the main causes of pollution, through the **burning** of **fossil fuels** for heating, transportation, and electricity. The main polluting gases include **carbon dioxide** (the pollutant responsible for the **greenhouse effect**) and sulfur and nitrogen dioxides (the pollutants responsible for **acid rain**). (*See also:* **Global warming**.)

Potential energy

The **energy** stored in objects and substances. Objects with stored energy have the ability, or potential, to do work. A coiled spring will uncoil if released. By uncoiling, it is doing work, so the coiled spring is said to have potential energy. A boulder on top of a cliff will fall down if it is pushed, so it also has potential energy. If a ball is held up, it has potential energy because, when it is let go, it falls

and releases energy.

Another form of potential energy is the electricity stored up as chemicals in a **battery** (*see:* **Chemical energy**).

Potential energy can be converted into energy of motion, or **kinetic energy**, and from this it can be turned into even more forms of energy. We see this when water is released from a reservoir. The water in the reservoir has potential energy. As it is released down chutes, the potential energy changes into energy of motion. The energy of motion then can turn **turbine** blades, which make electricity. The **electrical energy** produced can then be used to **power** a light bulb. In this way potential energy has been changed to motion energy, to electrical energy, and to **light** and **heat** energy. (*See also:* **Mechanical energy**.)

▲ **Potential energy**—This ball has potential energy because it is being held off the ground.

Power

The rate of doing work. In other words, the amount of work done in a certain time. A high-powered machine will do a certain amount of work faster than a low-powered machine. One of the most common units to measure power is the **watt**. The power of electrical appliances is rated in **watts**. Thus a 3kW heater will warm a room faster than a 2kW heater.

Power plant

A place designed to house **electric generators**. Power plants are often very large because they are designed to supply electricity to cities or large regions. Large generators tend to be more efficient than small ones.

A power plant needs a supply of **energy**. It can be in the form of natural **wind** or **water** energy, or it could be a **fuel** (stored energy). Of the fuels, **oil**, **coal**, **natural gas**, and **nuclear** fuel are by far the most important.

Electric generators that use fuel are usually **steam turbine** generators, meaning that the fuel is used to produce **heat** that turns water into **steam**. Jets of steam then make turbine blades rotate. The rotating blades are on one end of a shaft whose other end is connected to an electrical generator.

Because the conversion of energy to electricity is not efficient, large amounts of heat are produced during **power** generation. This heat has to be carried away by cooling water. In some cases the water

from rivers or the sea can be used directly, but in most cases the amount of water needed for direct cooling is larger than can be provided at the power plant. Cooling towers are built in which water supplies are contained. They act like giant radiators in cars. Water falling down the cooling towers is chilled by air. The cooled water is collected at the bottom of the towers and recycled.

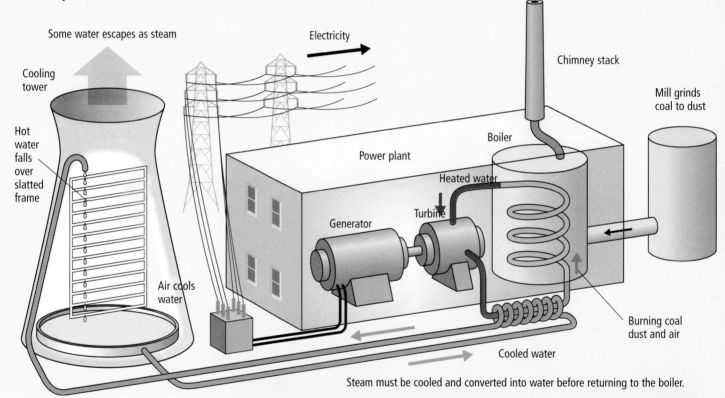

Some water escapes as steam

Electricity

Waste gases

Cooling tower

Chimney stack

Hot water falls over slatted frame

Mill grinds coal to dust

Boiler

Power plant

Heated water

Air cools water

Turbine

Generator

Burning coal dust and air

Cooled water

Steam must be cooled and converted into water before returning to the boiler.

Hot water from power plant

▲▶ **Power plant**—A thermal power plant requires a source of fuel such as gas, coal, (usually pulverized into a dust), or oil (sprayed as a mist into the boiler). The boiler is used to heat water which generates steam to turn the turbines of the generator.

A power plant is often located where it is convenient for the energy source it uses. Thus **hydroelectric power** plants are found on rivers or by reservoirs, and fossil fuel power plants are found near coal mines and **refineries**. That is because it is much cheaper to transport the electricity from the power plant than to transport the bulky and heavy (and therefore costly) raw materials to the power plant. Nuclear power plants are an exception to this and can be located near places where there is a demand because the amount of fuel they use is small. However, for safety reasons most are sited away from places where there are many people. (*See also:* **District heating**; **Electricity transmission**; **Pumped storage**.)

Pumped storage

It is not possible to store large amounts of electricity, and so it has to be generated to match instantaneous changes in demand. Pumped storage is a way of generating large amounts of electricity during times of peak demand using **hydroelectricity**.

During the course of any day the demand for electricity changes. It is lowest at night and highest at certain times of the day, such as when people are cooking. Large generators cannot, however, be turned up and down to meet this change in demand. As a result, they either have to run with spare generation for parts of the day, or some means has to be found to boost electricity at peak times.

In pumped storage water is pumped during the night to a high-level reservoir, perhaps at a natural site high up on a mountainside. This creates a supply of **potential energy**. The pumping uses electricity when there is spare generation. Then, at times of peak demand the water is released from the reservoir, turning the potential energy into movement (**kinetic**) **energy** that turns **turbines** and generates more electricity.

Modern pumped storage uses reversible-pump turbines. They are turbines that can be used as pumps when they are turned in one direction and generators when they turn in the opposite direction.

Pyrolysis

The heating of a substance so intensely that it is destroyed and converted into other substances. The **burning** of **fuels** is an example of pyrolysis.

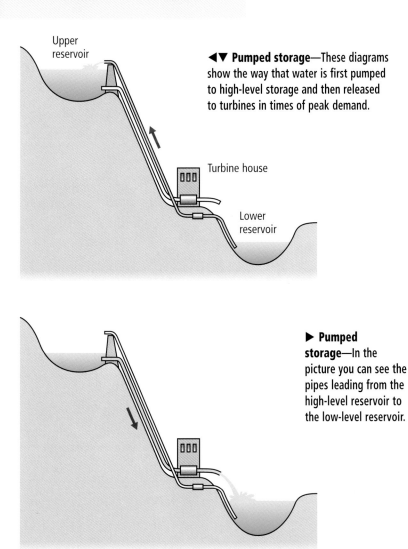

Upper reservoir

Turbine house

Lower reservoir

◄▼ Pumped storage—These diagrams show the way that water is first pumped to high-level storage and then released to turbines in times of peak demand.

► Pumped storage—In the picture you can see the pipes leading from the high-level reservoir to the low-level reservoir.

R

Radiant energy

Another term for **radiation**.

Refinery

A place where the mixture of substances called **crude oil** is distilled to extract them for use. (*See also:* **Petroleum**.)

Renewable energy

The general term for any form of **energy** that is the result of a recycling process rather than a one-way process such as the **burning** of **fossil fuel**.

Radiation

The process of sending **energy** from one place to another without the need for any conducting substance in between. The way that the **light** and **heat** energy from the Sun reaches the Earth through space is an example of radiation. Since there is no matter in space, energy could not reach the Earth if, as in **conduction** or **convection**, the energy needed a substance to transfer it.

Radiation is one of the three forms by which heat is exchanged. The others are conduction and convection (*see:* **Heat transfer**). The heat you feel from a fire is the result of radiation. A central heating radiator sends part of its heat into the air of a room by radiation (although radiators also warm by conduction and convection since the room is filled with air). The light you see from a **lamp** is the result of radiation.

Other forms of energy are also radiated. X-rays are a form of radiated light that cannot be seen. Radio waves are another example of energy being radiated that cannot be seen, heard, or felt.

The radiation of energy is often referred to by the word rays. Thus we say, "the rays of the Sun" or x-rays. (*See also:* **Electromagnetic radiation** and **Solar radiation**.)

▼ **Radiation**—A radiometer works on the principle that a black surface will absorb more radiant energy than a white one. As a result, a greater force is applied to the black surface. If the vanes are in a vacuum so that there is no air resistance, the radiant force is enough to spin the vanes.

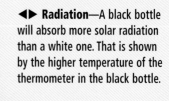

◄► **Radiation**—A black bottle will absorb more solar radiation than a white one. That is shown by the higher temperature of the thermometer in the black bottle.

The use of **water**, **wind**, **photosynthesis**, hot rocks, sun, and **tides** are all forms of renewable energy. Because these forms of **energy conversion** do not cause **pollution**, they are also often called "**green**" forms of energy.

As people began to worry about the environmental problems of the use of fossil fuels and the dwindling reserves of **oil** and **natural gas**, they began to look for alternative ways of producing energy that were not going to run out, and that were not harmful to the environment. Countries that did not have **petroleum** reserves were also eager to make sure that they were not dependent on other countries for their essential energy supplies.

People have become especially concerned about the effects of burning fossil fuels on the increased amount of **carbon dioxide** in the air and its relationship to **global**

warming and changing global weather patterns. These processes could, in turn, have a very serious effect on the frequency of natural disasters and the amount of crops that could be obtained from farmland.

Most industrialized countries have therefore begun programs to develop renewable energy systems with the goal of reducing their need for fossil fuels. The main ways that have been developed so far are those designed to make use of the energy in sunlight, in the wind, in moving water, and in the **heat** that naturally occurs below the ground.

Two ways have been found to make better use of the energy of sunlight (**solar power**). The first is to use photovoltaic cells, otherwise known as **solar cells**, which convert solar energy directly into electricity. They produce low-

voltage electricity very much as a **battery** does. The difficulty has been to develop photovoltaic cells that can produce enough **power** for widespread use. At the moment very large panels of cells are needed just to make small amounts of electricity.

The Sun has also been used directly to **heat** pipes carrying water, the water then being used to create **steam** that drives **turbines**.

Converting wind into electricity requires large wind generators, which when put together can produce substantial amounts of electricity. A large collection of wind generators is called a **wind farm**. They can only be located in places of reliable high winds and can be an eyesore.

The most reliable ways of using renewable energy so far developed are **hydroelectric power** and **geothermal energy**. In the case of hydroelectric power the power of moving water, often from a dam, is used to turn turbines directly. In the case of geothermal energy pipes are drilled into naturally hot rock, allowing steam to come to the surface and drive turbines.

The oceans contain enormous amounts of energy, but so far, except for a small number of tidal barrages, little has been achieved in harnessing this energy (*see:* **Ocean energy**).

Roast

To **heat** a material in air in such a way that many materials turn to gas and are given off. At the same time, solid materials combine with oxygen. This process, which is widely used for extracting metals from their ores, does not involve **combustion**. Calcium carbonate is roasted to produce lime, the raw material for cement.

▼ **Renewable energy**—Any sustainable energy form is a renewable energy resource—even wood-burning power plants. However, some forms of renewable energy may not be environmentally friendly because of possible pollution.

S

Sensible heat

The **energy** needed to cause the temperature of a substance to change when it is not at its boiling or **melting point**.

Smelting

The chemical process of heating an ore to a high enough temperature for the metal in it to melt. Smelting is widely used for extracting metals from their ores. A blast furnace is used for smelting iron ore. (*See also:* **Coke**.)

Smolder

A form of slow **combustion** without a **flame** and with the production of considerable amounts of smoke. (*See also:* **Charcoal**.)

Solar cell

A small device, also called a photovoltaic cell, that converts the **energy** in **light** into **electrical energy**. It relies on the fact that when light falls on some materials, they convert the light to electricity. A solar cell has no moving parts. Instead, it consists of specially prepared materials called semiconductors. Selenium was the first material to be used in this way.

Solar cells are sometimes called solar batteries. They can be gathered into groups called arrays to produce higher voltages and higher **power**. This allows them to be used as **electric generators**.

The electric power generated by this kind of cell is low for its size. On a small scale solar-cell panels can run individual machines or electronics, for example, remote weather stations and remote

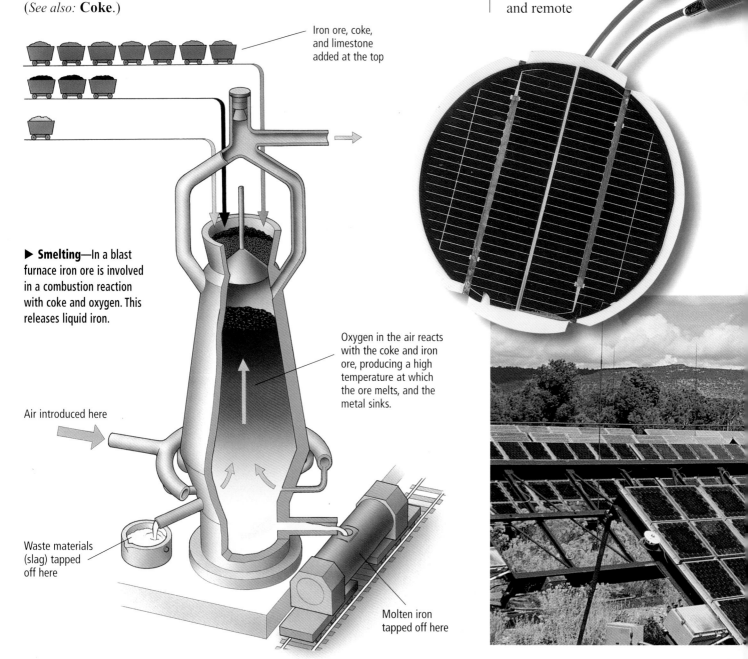

Iron ore, coke, and limestone added at the top

▶ **Smelting**—In a blast furnace iron ore is involved in a combustion reaction with coke and oxygen. This releases liquid iron.

Oxygen in the air reacts with the coke and iron ore, producing a high temperature at which the ore melts, and the metal sinks.

Air introduced here

Waste materials (slag) tapped off here

Molten iron tapped off here

lighting. Space satellites are also solar-cell powered, as are some hand-held calculators.

Solar power

The useful **energy** from sunshine. (*See:* **Solar cell** and **Solar thermal energy** for the two ways in which this energy can be converted.) (*See also:* **Solar radiation**.)

Solar radiation

Radiation from the Sun. Solar radiation is caused by a process called **fusion** that occurs deep within the Sun. This **energy** is released into space as **radiation**. The amount of radiation received by the Earth is a tiny fraction of the Sun's total radiation. Each square meter of the Earth receives 1.3 kilowatts of **solar power**, or about the same as a one-element electric heater.

About one-third of the **radiant energy** that reaches the atmosphere

◀▼ **Solar cell**—A solar cell (left) and a field of solar panels designed to produce more substantial electric output (below).

is reflected into space by clouds and the Earth's surface. The rest is used to power the atmosphere, the oceans, and life. Solar radiation provides the energy for the winds, thunderstorms, tornadoes, and hurricanes. It powers the Gulf Stream and other ocean currents. It also provides the energy needed for **photosynthesis**, the process that plants use to make tissues. And because animals rely on plants for their food, solar energy ultimately provides the energy for every living thing on Earth.

Sunshine is not received evenly over the Earth's surface. Only places where the Sun is directly overhead get the full amount stated above. When the Sun is lower in the sky, the amount of radiation received is less, and so the amount of solar energy varies with the time of day and also with the seasons. In the Northern Hemisphere the greatest amount of energy is received on June 21 (the summer solstice) and on December 21 in the Southern Hemisphere.

Whenever the Sun is not overhead, the glancing rays of **light**

spread out over a greater area and give less **heat** to each square meter. Places above the Arctic and Antarctic Circles get no solar radiation at all for part of the year.

The variation in sunshine energy has important effects. It means that places near the poles change in temperature between seasons far more than those near the equator. It also means that the energy for growth is far greater near the equator than near the poles. Additionally, it means that the chances of harnessing useful amounts of solar energy for conversion to electricity are much greater near the equator than they are near the poles.

The amount of useful solar radiation is not, however, just a matter of the angle of the sun. It also depends on the amount of cloud cover. Close to the equator the cloud cover is always high, and so the amount of sunshine received on the ground is always below its potential. For this reason the areas where solar energy can best be harnessed for use are in the subtropics, and specifically in desert lands.

Solar thermal energy

The **electrical energy** obtained by using sunlight to **heat** water and drive a **steam turbine**. Solar thermal heating is still in an experimental stage. It is used at a number of locations where there are large amounts of sunshine.

▶▼ **Solar thermal energy**—On this solar energy farm in California you can see the rows of parabolic mirrors that gather sunlight and focus it onto tubes carrying water (right). The water heats up to above 100°C, producing steam that can then be used to turn power-generating turbines. The power plant housing the generators can be seen in the background (below).

Tubes carrying water

Parabolic mirrors focus the Sun's rays on the tubes. The mirrors tilt as the Sun rises and falls through the day.

Power plant houses the generators. Computers control the tilt on the arrays of parabolic mirrors.

► **Spontaneous combustion**—Here (left) a cold liquid (ethylene glycol) is being added to a cold solid (potassium permanganate). At first nothing happens, but after some minutes spontaneous combustion (right) occurs. (No flame was added to cause this combustion.)

Ethylene glycol

Purple potassium permanganate crystals

Sound energy

A sound occurs when something disturbs an object, making it vibrate. This vibration then travels through the air, water, or a solid material. When it reaches our ears, it is heard as sound.

Sound is a mechanical vibration; so, although sound moves as a wave, it is quite unlike **light**. Sound cannot travel through space. It relies on the vibration of particles to carry it. (*See also:* **Conduction**.)

Sound is a form of movement (**kinetic**) **energy**. Because sound energy is small, the standard unit for measuring energy, the **joule** per second, is too large to use. In sound the common unit of measurement is the microjoule (a millionth of a **joule**). Sound energy is also called sound intensity.

Sound intensities can be compared on a scale. Each unit on the scale is 10 times larger or smaller than the unit above or below it. The sound intensity unit is called the bel (named for Alexander Graham Bell, 1847-1922) and is usually used in the form of a tenth of a bel, known as a decibel (dB). The quietest sound that can be heard is defined as 1dB. Sound becomes painful at 135dB.

Spontaneous combustion

When a combination of materials catches fire (combusts) without the use of a **flame** (*see:* **Combustion**). The chemical reaction involved is called oxidation.

Steam

The vapor that rises from water at its **boiling point**. Steam is invisible: What we normally call steam is actually a suspension of tiny water droplets inside the invisible water vapor.

▲ **Steam**—Steam is produced by boiling water. The steam is the invisible gas between the spout of the jug and the cloud of condensed droplets (often mistakenly called steam).

Steam engine, steam turbine

An engine that uses the **energy** of **steam** under pressure to drive machinery. In a steam engine water is heated in a closed boiler (a kind of pressure cooker) until the steam is under high pressure. Pressurized steam can do large amounts of work. The first steam engines were used to pump water out of mines. Later engines were used to provide the **power** for factories, steam locomotives, and many other machines. (*See also:* **Coal**.)

The modern forms of steam engines are called steam **turbines**. In a steam turbine high-pressure steam moves through a tube containing a type of propeller, the turbine. As the steam flows, it forces the turbine blades to rotate. Steam turbines are used to generate most of the world's electricity.

▼ **Steam engine/steam turbine**—Steam has been a source of power for centuries. One of the earliest uses was in steam trains. Modern power plants almost always use steam as the driving force for the turbines, no matter what fuel they burn.

T

Thermal decomposition

The breaking down of a material by heating. Anything that changes chemically when it is heated can be said to have decomposed. For example, when food is cooked, it changes composition. When a fire is lighted, the **fuel** decomposes into **steam** and other gases and small pieces of carbon (soot). When some chemicals are heated, they decompose into new compounds—this is the basis of some industrial processes.

Thermometer

A tool for measuring the temperature of a solid, liquid, or gas. Thermometers used to measure room temperature have a liquid confined in a narrow glass tube. The liquid is either alcohol or mercury. As the temperature rises, the liquid expands and moves higher in the tube. Because the **expansion** is the same for every unit rise in temperature, a simple

---

scale can be marked.

The Celsius (centigrade), Fahrenheit, and Kelvin scales all measure temperature in units of one degree. A degree on the Celsius (centigrade) and Kelvin scales is the same size. The Celsius scale begins with 0° as the **melting point** of water. The Kelvin scale begins with absolute zero; the melting point of water is 273°C on this scale. The Fahrenheit scale divides the difference between the melting and **boiling points** of water into 212 units rather than the 100 units of the other scales. Centigrade scale simply means a hundred-degree scale. It was renamed Celsius for the astronomer Anders Celsius (1701-1744). The Fahrenheit scale is named for Gabriel Fahrenheit (1686-1736), its inventor.

Tidal energy

The **energy** that can be gained by forcing the rising and falling tidal waters through **turbines**.

Tidal **power plants** can only be built where there is a large natural tidal range, such as in a funnel-

shaped estuary. If the estuary is blocked by a dam, then a reservoir of water can be built up on the inland side of the dam as the tide comes in. Water remains trapped in the estuary as the tide goes out, so that a head of water is formed between the trapped water and the sea. Eventually, the trapped water can be released through the turbines to generate electricity.

Few tidal plants have so far been built, in part because of the environmental disruption they cause. (*See also:* **Ocean energy**.)

Transformers

Two coils of wire on a shared iron core. They convert high-voltage to low-voltage electricity. The high-voltage side has more windings of wire than the low-voltage side. The ratio of the windings determines how much the voltage will be stepped up or down.

Transmission lines

The high-voltage cables used to carry **electrical energy** from **power plants** to where the electricity will be used, for example, in a town or city. (*See also:* **Electricity transmission** and **Utility pole**.)

Turbines

Machines resembling propellers that convert the movement (**kinetic**) **energy** in a liquid or gas into **mechanical energy**, which can turn the shaft of a **power** generator. (*See also:* **Electric generator**; **Power plant**; **Steam engine, steam turbine**.)

U

Utility pole

Wooden, metal, or concrete posts used to carry electricity cables.

◀ **Transmission lines**—Ceramic insulators are used to separate the cables from the metal of the transmission tower. Air is used as the insulator around the wire.

▼ **Transmission lines**—Electrical energy is carried across the country on high-voltage transmission lines like these.

V

Vaporization

The **change of state** from a liquid to a vapor at **boiling point**. (*See also:* **Heat of vaporization**.)

W

Water power

Any device that is able to convert the **kinetic** (movement) **energy** of flowing water into **mechanical** or **electrical energy**. **Waterwheels** were among the first powered machines. Modern waterwheels are called **turbines**, and they form part of **hydroelectric power plants.**

▲ **Water power**—The Industrial Revolution began with simple, direct water-powered machines such as the sawmill shown here.

Waterwheels

A wheel that converts the movement (**kinetic**) **energy** of flowing water into **mechanical energy** that will turn a shaft and work a machine. The earliest waterwheels were used to grind grain. They were soon adapted to saw timber, pump water, blow air into furnaces, and to **power** the looms in textile factories. It was the energy converted by waterwheels that helped start the Industrial Revolution. Indeed, so important were they as a source of energy, that the first factories were located in valleys with swiftly flowing rivers, even though they were sometimes far from towns and cities.

Watt

A unit of **power**. In electricity watt (W) is the power consumed and is calculated by multiplying the electrical current by the voltage. For example, a heater plugged into a wall socket at 110V that uses an electric current of 10A will consume $110 \times 10 = 1{,}100$W of **electrical power**.

Many electrical devices are rated in watts.

Wind farms

A group of wind **turbines** that are placed together in a location that has reliable and strong winds. The objective of grouping wind turbines is to produce a large amount of electricity in a single place so that it can be conveniently fed into an electricity supply. (*See also:* **Wind power**.)

▶ **Wind farms**—Wind farms use modern wind generators to produce electricity. This is more adaptable than direct use of mechanical energy from the wind.

Wind power

Any device that is able to convert the **kinetic** (movement) **energy** of the wind into **mechanical** or **electrical energy**. Windmills were some of the earliest powered machines. They were used for grinding grain and pumping water. Modern wind generators use huge propellerlike blades to turn the shaft of electrical generators and produce electrical energy (*see:* **Wind farms**).

The first windmills were designed in the same way as **waterwheels**. Later, it was discovered that the blades could be mounted either vertically or horizontally, leading to a greater variety of windmill design.

Because wind direction changes constantly, windmills with vertical blades had to be turned into the wind. The small "propeller" (fantail) seen sticking out of some windmills was designed to turn the windmill into the wind automatically.

▲ **Wind power**—Wind power has been used for centuries to grind grain and pump water.

Windmills also have to change the angle of their blades as the wind speed increases. That is because higher wind speeds can make the blades turn so fast that they could break away from their supporting towers. All windmills have a means of "feathering" their blades to prevent this problem.

Wood

(*See:* **Fuel wood**.)

Index